Maximising the
Profitability of Law Firms

For Pam, Mary and Amy
— whether they read it or not

Maximising the Profitability of Law Firms

Robert Mowbray, BSc, FCA

Partner, MacIntyre Hudson Chartered Accountants

BLACKSTONE
PRESS LIMITED

First published in Great Britain 1997 by Blackstone Press Limited,
9–15 Aldine Street, London W12 8AW. Telephone: 0181-740 2277

© R. Mowbray, 1997

ISBN: 1 85431 597 8

British Library Cataloguing in Publication Data
A CIP catalogue record for this book is available from the British Library.

Typeset by Montage Studios Ltd, Tonbridge, Kent
Printed by Livesey Ltd, Shrewsbury, Shropshire

Contents

Preface   vii

1 Introduction   1

2 The Starting Point — Solicitors' Accounts   3

Faldo Woosnam Lyle

3 The Keys to Profitability and Rules of Thumb   9

Earnings of equity partners — Significance of accounting policies

4 Business Plans — Development, Involvement and Understanding 16

Reasons why firms go bust — Preparing a master budget — Annual budgets
— Fee income budget — Professional staff costs budget — Overheads budget
— What happens when the budgets have been set?

**5 The Mechanics of Profitability — Gearing, Chargeable Hours,
Charge-out Rates, Recovery and Margin**   35

Gearing — Chargeable hours — Charge-out rates — Recovery — Margin —
Gearing, chargeable hours, charge-out rates, recovery and margin – who
influences performance? — Industry averages for gearing — Industry averages
for chargeable hours — Industry averages for charge-out rates — Industry
averages for recovery — Margin

Contents

6   Working Capital Control   56

7   Investment Appraisal   62

8   Management Reporting   65

9   The Development of Personal and Management Skills   72

Introduction — Significance of partners' management skills — What specific
skills are needed?

10   The Role of Client Care in Profitability   88

Reviewing reality — Internal communications — Attending seminars —
Training partners and staff — Pricing — Marketing methods

11   Tax Planning — Keeping the Profits   106

Work in progress valuation — Borrowing — Deciding on the right year end for
tax purposes – self assessment — Service companies — Retirement planning
in solicitors' partnerships — Identification of non-professional or trading
income — Capital gains tax and retirement relief — Inheritance tax and
business property relief

Index   130

Preface

This book seeks to provide a clear explanation of why some firms manage to earn high profits and others don't. Having established some fundamental rules on profitability and some benchmarks for establishing performance levels, the text then provides detailed and practical advice on the steps which need to be taken to improve profitability.

The analysis of profitability encompasses the development of personal and management skills, the role of client care in profitability and the development of realistic business plans.

Having established how to improve the financial management and profitability of firms, the book also provides ideas on tax planning to ensure that as much as possible of the hard earned profits remain in the pockets of the partners.

Robert Mowbray
December 1996

1

Introduction

This book should be of interest to anyone who is considering a career in the legal profession or who is already in the profession. Indeed, it may also be of interest to people who have completed their careers and who wish to look back upon their achievements and measure their success.

The book will be of particular use to managing or senior partners of a firm who are trying to develop a framework for their role and who wish to be able to put in place more rigid mechanisms for ensuring that levels of profitability are achieved. Aspiring partners should find the book of interest because in the commercial world in which firms operate today new partners are only going to be appointed if they have both legal skills and commercial awareness in everything that they do. Trainees and law students should also read and understand the book so that before even entering the profession they have a clear understanding of what they need to do to ensure that they are successful in a professional career.

The book may of course be of interest to people who deal with firms of solicitors. While not all firms will like their clients to read the book, if clients do read and understand the book then it should be possible for better relationships to be formed between firms and their clients. Accountants who work with solicitors and who report on solicitors' accounts may also find the book useful as will bankers who provide finance for so many firms.

Introduction

Before embarking on the book it may be useful to consider the best way of obtaining maximum benefit from the book. For most people it is probably right to read the book quickly, but completely, to get an overview of the content before going back into specific areas that are of particular interest to the reader. It would be slightly dangerous to read chapters in isolation since most of the chapters overlap and interlink to a greater or lesser extent and a complete picture will only be obtained by reading the entire book.

The book contains industry information on law firms which should be invaluable to individual fee earners and to firms as a whole. It is extremely difficult to give norms given the range of size and of type of firms that operate. Most of the information that is given in the book relates to the medium to larger firms because any wild distortions which may exist in smaller firms are smoothed out through the averages obtained from larger firms with larger numbers of fee earners. The information contained in the book is accurate and up to date at the time of publication but, like all professions and like industry, we are in a period of rapid change and many of the norms that are highlighted may well change significantly in the coming years. Where such change is anticipated it has been highlighted.

It is extremely difficult to get hold of specific information on individual firms as a great deal of secrecy still surrounds the financial results of professional practices. Incorporation looms for many professional firms and only with incorporation will full financial disclosure become mandatory for most firms.

2

The Starting Point — Solicitors' Accounts

The starting point in any review of profitability will probably be a review of the most recent financial statements prepared for a particular firm. Such a review may be undertaken by a managing partner, any partner within the firm who is minded to do so or indeed by new or potential partners who wish to have a better understanding of the firm.

Before reading any further through the book it may be worth testing the existing level of knowledge. This can probably best be done by considering the accounts of Faldo Woosnam Lyle which appear below. It would be useful to note down answers to the questions raised at this stage and then to compare answers later once the book has been thoroughly read.

Faldo Woosnam Lyle

You have just been appointed managing partner of the firm. The firm is based in one large office in Northampton, with an office in Brussels which was opened in 1991. You are an experienced solicitor, and you are held in high regard by your partners because of your business acumen.

It is now 1 August 1996 and you are reviewing the accounts and sundry information that is available for the year that ended on 30 April 1996.

After your review, you hope to implement changes which will improve the profitability of the firm.

You are to review the information and list out the following:

    (a)   The financial strengths of the firm.
    (b)   The financial weaknesses of the firm.
    (c)   The management information that you believe should be provided to all fee earners.

Faldo Woosnam Lyle
Balance Sheet
30 April 1996

	1996 £'000		1995 £'000
FIXED ASSETS	1,050		650
INVESTMENTS			
Investment in Brussels office at cost	265		265

CURRENT ASSETS				
Debtors	5,140		3,927	
Work in Progress	4,260		3,051	
Sundry debtors and prepayments	630		580	
Cash in hand	7		2	
	10,037		7,560	

CURRENT LIABILITIES				
Bank overdraft	6,400		4,300	
Sundry creditors	1,750		1,800	
Counsel's fees	550		375	
	8,700		6,475	

NET CURRENT ASSETS		1,337		1,085
NET ASSETS		£2,652		£2,000
CAPITAL ACCOUNTS		2,500		2,000
CURRENT ACCOUNTS		152		—
		£2,652		£2,000

Faldo Woosnam Lyle
Profit and Loss Account
30 April 1996

	1996 £'000		1995 £'000
Turnover	20,173		15,562
Office expenditure	15,607		11,672
Operating profit	4,566		3,890
Other income			
Commissions receivable	58	73	
Interest earned	126	142	
Brussels office	180	135	
	364		350
Profit for allocation	£4,930		£4,240

Faldo Woosnam Lyle
Office Expenditure
30 April 1996

	1996 £'000	1995 £'000
STAFF EXPENSES		
Salaries and NIC	8,146	6,048
Staff welfare and canteen	214	186
Car provision	107	65
Recruitment fees	327	164
Pension contributions	311	227
Private patients plan	20	16
Training	152	127
Practising certificates	45	36
Subscriptions	6	8
	9,328	6,877
ACCOMMODATION EXPENSES		
Amortisation of lease	58	58
Repairs and renewals	192	227
Rent	1,370	820
Rates	367	339
Depreciation — furniture & equipment	65	58
Insurance	40	44
Maintenance — computer	24	32
Light and heat	55	47
Cleaning	72	71
Postage	45	41
Telephone, telex & fax	286	236
Photocopying	35	30
Printing and stationery	165	121
Brochures	43	8
Books and journals	74	56
Sundries	3,388	2,607
	6,279	4,795
TOTAL	£15,607	£11,672

Faldo Woosnam Lyle
Sundries
30 April 1996

	1996 £'000	1995 £'000
SUNDRIES		
Newspapers	5	4
Entertainment	183	114
Partners' expense allowance	249	186
Professional indemnity insurance	740	765
PR consultancy	224	85
Accountancy and taxation	248	176
Bank charges	52	49
Bank interest	1,031	960
Travel	219	56
Bad debts	437	212
	£3,388	£2,607

OTHER INFORMATION

EQUITY PARTNERS	35	33
SALARIED PARTNERS (cost included in staff expenses)	6	6

AVERAGE CHARGEABLE HOURS		
Partners	1,150	1,150
Assistants	1,250	1,250
Trainee solicitors	1,100	1,100

CHARGE-OUT RATES		
Partners	165–250	150–225
Assistants	95–150	85–135
Trainee Solicitors	55–75	50–70

ACCOUNTING POLICIES
Work in progress @ 80% of charge-out rate value
Debts written off when over 6 months old

3

The Keys to Profitability and Rules of Thumb

Earnings of equity partners

The starting point in the search to understand how firms maximise their profitability must be to establish exactly how much an equity partner should earn in a particular firm. Most partners will be able to tell you very quickly how much they do earn but very few have rationalised how much they should earn. The range of profitability in UK law firms, on average per equity partner, extends from losses to profits in excess of £400,000 per partner.

To understand why such wide ranges of profitability can appear it is important to understand some fundamental rules. Figure 1 shows the normal position for a professional firm that is operating successfully. This rule of thumb has been used by the best firms over the last 100 years.

Figure 1   Rule of thumb — professional firm profitability

	£
Fee income	100
Professional staff costs	(33)
Gross profit	67
Overheads	(34)
Net profit	£33

For every £100 of fee income, whether the fee income be £100,000, £1 million or £100 million, it is possible to earn a percentage of that income as net profit if the practice is run efficiently. To achieve 33% net profit, which is the goal for most firms, it is necessary to restrict costs to 67% of fee income. The simple rule of thumb which is explained in Figure 1 shows that one third of fee income will disappear in professional staff costs with a further one third going in overheads.

The figure for professional staff costs includes the cost of all fee earner salaries and associated costs, together with the cost of salaried or fixed share partners, since the profit percentage of 33% relates just to the equity partner share. Firms which structure themselves with a large number of salaried partners may find that professional staff costs exceed 33% and therefore the net profit percentage drops but this is more than compensated for by the far larger fee income that is controlled by each equity partner.

When the constituent parts of overheads are considered there is a vast array of costs which can be incurred. While any cost may be large in monetary terms there are normally two costs which account for a large percentage of the total overheads figure. These two overheads are premises costs and support staff costs. A rule of thumb for premises costs is that these costs should be about 10% of fee income. If the costs are much less than this then perhaps the quality of the premises will not attract the right sorts of clients for the future and if much more than this is spent on premises then perhaps the cost becomes disproportionate to the fees being earned. For example, if the firm is spending 20% of its gross fees on premises costs then, instead of being able to earn a net profit percentage of 33%, it would only be able to earn a net profit percentage of 23% until such time as new premises could be obtained or until such time as fee income could grow sufficiently to bring premises costs down to just 10% of fee income.

It can be seen from Figure 1 therefore that the greatest constraint on profitability in firms is the size of fees being billed per equity partner. Figure 2 gives more up to date information on the fees of some of the major firms together with the number of partners and the reported profits earned per equity partner. When looking at Figure 2, you should note that if the total fee income of any firm is divided by the number of partners this gives the fee income per partner. If 33% of this figure is taken then this is the potential profit that could be earned by the firm. While there are a few firms who achieve a percentage in excess of this level this is likely to be a one-off result in a particular year due to one or more sizeable corporate transactions that have distorted the results. For the majority of firms, however, the percentage reported for net profit is less than 33% and this will be because there is not perfect efficiency within the firm. Some firms achieve a net profit percentage in excess of 33% of fee income because there are a number of salaried partners. In these circumstances salaried partners are contributing extra profit to the equity partners of the firm.

Figure 2   Profitability of firms

Firm	Fee income £'millions	Number of partners	Fees per partner £'000	Profit per equity partner £'000
1 Clifford Chance	230	224	1,026	293
2 Linklaters & Paines	173	154	1,123	348
3 Freshfields	138	141	979	294
4 Allen & Overy	127.5	123	1,037	395
5 Slaughter & May	126	102	1,235	395
6 Lovell White Durrant	115	143	804	243
7 Herbert Smith	78	105	743	210
8 Simmons & Simmons	74	122	607	226
9 Norton Rose	68	99	687	181
10 Dibb Lupton Bromhead	56.5	123	459	200

Source: *Legal Business*, September 1995

Average profitability in firms is somewhere in the range of 20%–25% of fee income. Very small practices and in particular sole practitioners trading from their own premises or from home may achieve a higher percentage but this is often due to the fact that there is no true premises cost in the accounts or that perhaps there are not yet any staff. Even though the percentages are higher than 33%, the profit figure in monetary firms would be much lower than for larger firms because the gross fees that can be handled by a sole practitioner or a smaller firm will be far less for each partner than is the case in a larger firm.

Surveys of firms of similar size and trading in the same location often show that profits on average per equity partner vary by two or threefold between firms.

Given that these firms are trading in the same area and are of comparable size and the fee income per equity partner is probably comparable, the reason for the variation in profit is simply because the net profit percentage varies by this factor across a range of similar firms.

Significance of accounting policies

Having developed some principles for how profitability can be measured, it is now important to understand that it is possible to manipulate the reported profits of a firm and hence its net profit percentage quite dramatically simply by altering various accounting policies that the firm uses in the preparation of its accounts. The following four are examples of accounting policies in law firms that can result in significant distortions.

Bad debts

When a firm issues a bill, it recognises income in its profit and loss account and hence profit. However, the writing off of a debt or the provision that is made against a doubtful debt is an expense in the accounts, but the point at which a bad debt is recognised varies considerably from firm to firm. Many lawyers do not provide against bad debt until the debtor is declared bankrupt or becomes insolvent, while other firms may provide against a bad debt once it is more than a certain number of months old, for example over 6 months or 12 months old. This difference in policy will mean that potentially a debt could be written off in one year rather than another and hence will lead to a change in the profits in one year as opposed to another. While this has no overall effect on the firm, or on the partners within the firm, it does affect the individual partners in each year and if there is a change of partnership then, potentially, profits are shifted from one group of partners to another.

Work in progress

The range of accounting policies used for the valuation of work in progress is enormous and with the scale of figures often involved leads to some quite dramatic differences between firms. The range is from showing work in progress at nil value in the accounts through to showing work in progress at full charge-out rate value. A couple of examples will serve to illustrate the potential problems that can arise from this range of accounting policies.

Consider a firm whose policy for valuing work in progress is to value it at full chargeable value provided that bills are issued for work in progress within 3 months of the year end. This will encourage partners in any year to make sure that as much work in progress as possible is billed immediately after the year end, even if the client does not settle that bill for many months afterwards. Suppose a firm manages to bill 80% of its work in progress within 3 months of the end of the year, then it will value its work in progress at 80% of full value and this will lead to extra profit within the firm compared with a firm that does not include work in progress in the profit and loss account. As can be seen in Figure 3, a problem which may arise for a firm that has this accounting policy is that if these profits which are being reported are then distributed to partners, the firm may end up with a significantly large bank overdraft. As Figure 3 shows, without the accounting policy for work in progress which values it at full chargeable value, the work in progress figure would be £25 million less and if these profits are not being distributed the borrowings are £25 million less, which would put the firm in a more stable financial position.

Figure 3   Undercapitalisation

	Firm A £'000	Firm B £'000	(with work in progress)
Balance sheet			
Fixed assets	3,000	3,000	
Current assets			
Work in progress	—	25,000	
Debtors	20,000	20,000	
Bank balance	2,000	—	
Current liabilities			
Creditors	(15,000)	(15,000)	
Bank overdrafts	—	(23,000)	
Net assets	£10,000	£10,000	
Partners' capital	£10,000	£10,000	

Another firm might value work in progress at a figure of zero or as close to zero as possible. The benefit of such a basis of valuation is that profits are understated and hence less tax is paid. If tax payments are deferred in this way then the firm can retain more cash to fund its expansion rather than having to go to the banks or to partners to obtain such capital. However, imagine the situation where a firm has an enormous amount of work in progress, perhaps as much as a whole year's fees in hand at the year end. Under such circumstances the existing partners will not have recognised to date the value of that work in progress in the accounts and hence will not have shared in the profit that has been created. It is highly unlikely that a partner in this firm would ever want to leave because he would be leaving behind his share of the work in progress. Conversely, a partner who had worked in the first sort of firm discussed would love to walk away from the virtually insolvent practice and become a partner in the new firm. The partner has taken all of the profit out of the first firm and could now join the new firm and be in a position to bill out further profit without actually doing any work, by simply using up the existing work in progress mountain.

Depreciation

As most firms do not buy their own premises the largest item of capital expenditure in most firms is computer equipment and information technology (IT). If one went back 10 years, one would have found that most firms depreciated their IT expenditure over a relatively long period of perhaps 5 or 10 years, thus spreading the capital cost over a reasonable number of years. However, policies have changed recently and now it is more common to find firms writing off a large amount of their IT expenditure in one year with other items being written off over periods of up to 3 years. This means that the cost of computer equipment is being written off far faster and hence potentially partners could suffer more of a shock in any one year. In professional life one will more regularly come across new partners in firms who wish that they had become a partner a year later simply because they discovered to their horror that the office was completely rekitted with computer technology in the year in which they became a partner rather than the year before they became a partner. Equally in such a firm there will be partners who are made up in the following year who are delighted to find that their appointment was delayed by a year because they have not shared in the suffering of the capital cost of kitting out the office with new technology.

Deferred revenue expenditure

While this is not a policy that is adopted by many firms at present it seems likely that it may be considered by more firms in the future. The principle of the policy is best understood by thinking about the estate agency industry in its boom period of the early to mid 1980s. During this period estate agency businesses knew that the only way to expand their profits quickly was to open new offices and hence to attract more work. The downside of opening a new office was that while no income arose through house completions for approximately 6 months, costs were incurred from the first day such as the renting of the new agency and the payment of staff salaries. A policy developed whereby many agencies capitalised the running costs of the first 6 months and put these costs in the balance sheet, rather than the profit and loss account, with a view to writing these costs off against the income stream which followed over perhaps the next 5 years.

Lawyers might wish to pursue a similar policy, either when opening a new office or indeed when developing a new department or specialism within an existing office. Without such a policy it might well be that the older partners would veto such a development because, in their eyes, they would only pay for the costs of setting up and would not be around to share in the profits that follow. However, if the project were ultimately to be profitable it would be a shame if it were vetoed and hence the spreading of the initial costs of starting a new operation over a longer period should be allowed to happen if this would lead to the right decision in the medium to long term.

These are just a few of the accounting policies that can affect the accounts of a law firm. There are many others that can be tinkered with but others are unlikely to affect the reported results to the same extent as those discussed above. The point about accounting policies is that there is not perfect consistency in the way that firms prepare their accounts. It is therefore always important to ensure that one is comparing like with like when interpreting the results of two different firms or two different accounting periods of the same firm.

4

Business Plans — Development, Involvement and Understanding

Every firm of solicitors, just like every business, needs to develop business plans which provide focus to the business and measures of performance for the partners and staff who work in the firm. Historically a large majority of firms have had no written medium to long term aims and a large number of these have had no detailed annual budgets in place. While the position has certainly improved in recent years, the quality of such plans is still severely lacking in the majority of firms. If one looks at corporate clients of firms it is often only too obvious which clients are going to grow and become increasingly profitable. One of the main factors that leads to increasing profits is whether or not the business has in place sound business plans that are managed and monitored. Businesses and firms that do not have budgets normally simply survive from year to year without making any significant strides forwards.

Before considering in some detail the way in which these budgets can be put together, it is worth stopping for a moment and appreciating just how vulnerable a professional firm is to external influences and to realise that even the most successful firm could get into severe financial trouble relatively quickly. Numerous surveys have been undertaken on businesses that have failed and become insolvent. The following is a list of the major contributory factors that have been highlighted in these surveys and under each heading there is information which explains how this may be relevant to a professional firm.

Reasons why firms go bust

Poor management control

If the partners of a firm stop and anticipate why they may get into severe financial trouble they will usually consider a number of external factors which they believe are outside their control. While these external factors may ultimately be outside their control there is certainly something that can be done to protect against each and every one of these factors. The important thing is to spot what is happening as early as possible so that action can be taken as quickly as possible. The vast majority of business managers who have suffered insolvency have, with hindsight, highlighted the major reason for their insolvency as being their own poor financial management. The other items appearing in this list are largely to do with external factors but this does not mean that they cannot be managed.

Undercapitalisation

Businesses with insufficient capital may get into serious financial trouble particularly when starting up but also during periods of expansion following a recession. This problem is relevant to a law firm in that any new firm that is starting up will only have a certain amount of partner capital. If more investment is required initially for information technology, equipment, premises etc. and it takes a little longer than was expected to issue bills to clients and collect cash from them, then a firm may get into trouble before it has really started. Perhaps of greater concern in the medium and larger sized firms is what happens after a recession. The recent recession has left many firms in a far weaker financial state than they were in prior to the recession. The turning of the corner and the growth once again of fee income will be a huge relief to many firms. The danger, however, is that too much work is taken on too quickly. From the moment work is taken on, costs start to be incurred, but as will be discussed in more detail later on it is often many months before any cash will be received from a client. The danger therefore is that while the firm is growing and making profits it never survives to see these profits because it becomes insolvent before the cash is received.

Gross profit level is too low

In Figure 1 we looked at the standard model for profitability within a solicitors' firm. The target for net profit of 33% of fee income can only be achieved with a gross profit of 67%. Gross profit is calculated as the difference between fee income and professional staff costs. The gross profit is the profit that is made from direct trading before overheads are taken into account. The professional firm is maybe better understood if one considers professional staff costs as those which are bought in by a firm and the time that these people create as the income which is sold to clients to create a gross profit. What is the effect of a fall in gross profit from 67% to 66%? A fall in margin does not necessarily affect overheads in any way and therefore one percentage point could flow down to the bottom of the profit and loss account changing the targeted net profit of 33% to 32% or a more typical net profit percentage of 25% down to 24%. For an average firm, this fall from 25% to 24% equates to a 4% drop in profits. In other words the rule of thumb for a solicitor is that a fall of 1% in the margin will affect profits by 4% and therefore a fall of 5% in the margin will affect profits by 20% and a 10% fall in the margin will affect profits by 40%. Profitability is therefore extremely volatile and it is important to measure the margins that have been earned.

Historically, before the development of information technology within firms it would have been unusual to find a firm that could tell you about the levels of profit that were being earned in various departments. There is little excuse for this today, although many firms still choose to produce management information for the firm as a whole, rather than breaking it down into departmental results for the fear that such information will be divisive. Such a mentality is extremely dangerous in the competitive world that exists today. Firms must understand the different margins that are being earned in different areas of work and ensure that more resources are put into highly profitable areas and that the firms correct or back out of areas earning lower margins. If a firm waits to understand what is happening in the market place by reading about it in the professional press then it will react too slowly. The name of the game is to spot what is happening in the market place before competitors and to take the appropriate action.

If the gross profit margin in a particular firm is reviewed, one often finds that the gross profit margin in various departments may vary from 50% to 75% with an average of 63%. Without this information the partners and fee earners would not have been aware of such a diversity. A department with a lower gross profit margin is not necessarily performing worse in overall terms than one with a higher gross profit margin. External factors do affect the margins and over a period of time economic factors tend to help some departments rather than others. For example, most property lawyers would say that during the 1980s the margins that were earned on property work increased steadily and finally peaked in the late 1980s before crashing quite quickly in the early 1990s. By the middle of the 1990s the margins had begun to pick up but nobody yet knows whether the margins will return to the heights of the late 1980s once again. In contrast many litigators found that margins during the 1980s were only moderate but that during the early 1990s these margins rocketed particularly in certain types of litigation. There were signs by the mid 1990s that perhaps in many areas of litigation the margins were beginning to decline while the margins in some types of litigation remained extremely high.

A medium sized firm which has established a number of departments is perhaps a little more stable because by having departments that operate in different sectors it is able to cushion poor performance in one department by average or above average performance in another.

If one ever asks fee earners what margin they are achieving during a particular week it is highly unlikely that they can give a clear answer just by sitting at a desk. It is impossible to say whether one is operating at a 66% margin or a 60% margin or a 63% margin. Movements of over 10% may become recognisable but as this equates to a movement in profitability of 40%, perhaps this is recognising things a little too late.

High interest rates

Interest rates have become extremely volatile over the last two decades with large fluctuations in rates over relatively short periods of time. Firms that have borrowed excessively from banks to finance capital expenditure and working capital will therefore suffer variable interest charges unless the finance has been obtained at fixed rates. In planning for the future, it is particularly important to consider movements in interest rates and the effect that this will have on cash flow and profitability.

In recent years interest rates have fallen dramatically and they now appear to be more stable but this is not necessarily going to remain true forever.

Excessive diversification

Historically, management textbooks have advised that businesses should diversify with a view to spreading risk. There are many businesses which have diversified extensively over the last 20 years. The theme in the early 1990s has been one of divestment rather than diversification with businesses going back to their core activities. The risk of over diversification is perhaps particularly acute within a law firm because of the usually limited amount of management time that is available. For example, if a firm opens a new office or opens a new department, the managing partners who are often significant fee earners in their own right, will have to use part of their limited time to manage this development. The core activities in the main departments that have already been established may suffer, and tiny movements in the margin on core activities could have a significant effect on the overall profitability of firms.

The other difficulty with diversification is not understanding the business as well as your new competitors. A good example of this problem in the future will be the whole subject of multi-disciplinary firms. What exactly is going to happen over the coming years? Will law firms acquire accountancy firms or will accountancy firms acquire law firms? If a law firm acquires another law firm there are clearly risks but at least the business that is being taken on is extremely similar to the business that is already being run. However, if a law firm acquires an accountancy firm, while there may be many similarities there are also some fundamental differences between the two types of firms and there would be significant risk for the new owners. It is apparent therefore that a certain amount of diversification will spread risk by enabling the firm to operate in a range of markets, but over diversification is always going to be a significant risk to a firm.

Preparing a master budget

The question often asked within a firm is the period that should be covered by the financial budgets. The most usual answer is that they should be produced for a year, but perhaps the fuller answer should be that detailed budgets should be prepared for a year but that there should be some longer term master plan or budget in place which leads to the development of detailed annual budgets. Ten years ago firms that produced master budgets might well have produced budgets for a 5–10 year period. In recent years, however, change has been so dramatic within firms that it is probably now unrealistic to try to prepare master plans for more than 3–5 years and for most firms 3 years is probably sufficient. Many lawyers fail to appreciate just why such a budget is important. The purpose of this budget is to bring into focus what is to be achieved in the medium to long term as opposed to the short term. The failure to produce budgets of this sort will probably mean that firms will simply survive rather than make fundamental change and steady growth over a number of years.

In preparing a master budget there are a number of parties who have to be considered if the final budget is going to be achievable. The first interested party is the equity partners and this is perhaps the most obvious party. It is probably also right to include within this party the thoughts of salaried partners and also of bankers where significant financing is provided by a bank to the firm. The second party who has to be considered is the firm's clients because if the firm fails to deliver the right level of service to clients over a period of time then the firm itself will not achieve its targets as it will not maintain existing clients, let alone attract new clients. Within this book it has already been established that the greatest limiting factor on profitability in firms is the size of the fee portfolio per equity partner.

The final group of people who must be considered in the preparation of a master budget are the employees of the firm. Most partners recognise that staff loyalty ultimately leads to higher levels of profit because with high staff turnover it is impossible to deliver client service with the same degree of efficiency. During the recession of the early 1990s, many managing partners became only too aware of the importance of staff loyalty. During this period, clients became more and more cost conscious and forced prices down for many types of work. If, during this period, there had been a high turnover of staff then firms would have found it far more difficult to survive and make reasonable levels of profit. However, during this time staff turnover dropped dramatically and this staff loyalty meant that reasonable profit levels could normally be maintained. The danger at the end of the recession when work volumes pick up is that staff will start to move again and while there is more work the profitability on that work reduces because of the lack of staff loyalty.

Within many firms the partners will go away for a weekend every 1–2 years to try to review this master plan and to assess whether what they are doing is still valid. The budgets produced on such occasions by partners are often unachievable simply because all three parties listed above have not been considered. It is extremely easy to produce a plan that will make you the most profitable firm in the history of the legal profession. It is quite another thing to achieve it.

An example of a master budget for a firm follows in Figure 4 to provide some information on how such a budget could be constructed. The example is just to illustrate some main headings that might be used and individual firms must decide exactly how such a budget is to be prepared. It is extremely important that, in preparing such a budget, a firm takes on board the views of the entire partnership and, where appropriate, of members of staff. Many larger firms have produced very detailed budgets simply through the consultation of a number of senior partners. This may or may not be accepted by the other partners but it is highly unlikely that a master budget will ever be achieved unless there is acceptance amongst all of the other partners of that budget and the required role of each and every partner.

When preparing the budget it is probably therefore right to try to do so over a period of time rather than at just one meeting, since it is something that is always evolving.

Figure 4   Master budget — example

ABC & Co.
3 Year Plan to 31 December 19X8
Prepared & Agreed 26 January 19X6

1.   Solvency
(i)   The firm will not allow bank overdrafts to exceed 50% of partners' capital. Drawings will be restricted if necessary to ensure that this is achieved in order to ensure that over reliance is not placed on bank finance.
(ii)   Undistributed profits caused by the rule in (i) above will normally be used to increase partners' capital. The main reason for increased partner capital over the period of this plan is to finance the increased working capital (work in progress and debtors) that will be necessary for the budgeted increase in fee income.
(iii)   Working capital control needs to be improved. At present it takes on average 120 days from receiving an instruction to issuing a bill and a further 110 days on average before cash is received. The total credit given to clients of 230 days on average is to be reduced to 180 days over the next 3 years.
(iv)   New computers and office equipment will be leased to spread the cash cost over the life of the lease.
(v)   Drawing will be allowed at 70% of budgeted profits, any balance on current accounts being settled 3 months after the year end.

2.   Profitability
(i)   The gross profit percentage being achieved by the firm is currently 64%. The intention is to increase this figure to 67% over the next 3 years. An analysis by department is shown below:

Department	Current gross profit %	Gross profit % By 31.12.X8
Commercial property	60%	64%
Private client	56%	60%
Litigation	71%	70%
Company commercial	68%	70%
Overall	64%	67%

(ii)   The net profit percentage of the firm is at present 28%. It is intended to increase this to 31% by 31 December 19X8.

(iii) The average profit share per equity partner is to be increased over the next 3 years as follows:

Year	Average profit share £
19X6	100,000
19X7	115,000
19X8	130,000

3.   Fee growth/market share

(i)   Current average fee levels per partner are to be increased over the next 3 years as follows:

Year	Average fee per partner £
19X6	350,000
19X7	380,000
19X8	420,000

(ii)   It is anticipated that 50% of the increase in fees will come from existing clients providing further instructions with the balance coming from new clients.

(iii) Partners are to attempt to attract a larger client size on average as such larger clients usually provide a higher level of profit. Each partner is to try to attract a client with recurring fees in excess of £25,000 per annum in each of the next 3 years.

4.   Productivity

(i)   Fee earner to support staff ratios are to be changed from an existing ratio of 45% fee earners to 55% non fee earners to a new mix with 60% fee earning staff. This is to be achieved by 31 December 19X8 but will only be achieved if all fee earners have a terminal on their desk by this date.

(ii) The number of fee earners per partner is to be increased from 1.5 to 2.5 over the period to 31 December 19X8. The increase will represent further assistant solicitors and legal executives: there will be no more trainees than at present.

(iii) The property and litigation departments will seek to use a higher proportion of legal executives and paralegals in the work undertaken. At present both departments just use trainees and assistant solicitors.

5. Staff development

(i) The firm aims to reduce fee earner staff turnover to 15% per annum and support staff turnover to 20% by 31 December 19X8. At present the comparable figures are 25% and 33% respectively. It is believed that a lower level of staff turnover will provide a higher level of productivity and profitability.

(ii) A profit related pay scheme is to be established for all staff by 31 December 19X6.

(iii) Life assurance and private health insurance are to be provided to all fee earners by 31 December 19X7.

(iv) The training budget is to be increased to 5% of salary costs and this amount will be spent in each of the next 3 years.

(v) The staff partner will review the induction procedures for new staff and issue revised guidance by 30 June 19X6.

(vi) The appraisal system will be reviewed and implemented on a 6 monthly basis for all staff from 30 September 19X6.

(vii) The partners will issue a statement to staff by 31 March 19X6 which outlines the commitment to developing staff. This statement will be developed in consultation with a cross section of staff.

Figure 5 explains the usual annual financial cycle that exists within a business and indeed within a law firm. The cycle consists of the preparation of annual budgets, the preparation of management information throughout the year and the final preparation of annual accounts at the end of the year. If we consider this cycle again within a law firm a number of matters arise.

Figure 5 Annual financial cycle

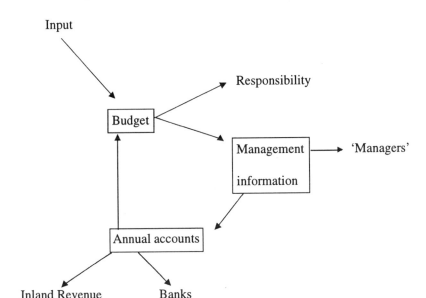

It is extremely important to ensure that all partners are involved in the setting of budgets. Smaller firms often do not bother with budgets because they believe it to be an unnecessary burden and in larger firms the creation of budgets is often left to the in-house accountant. If an in-house accountant is asked to produce a budget then all that can be used is the historical data which, if the trend is continued, will lead to a certain budget. While this might be interesting, it is never going to be as precise as a budget that is created with input from each of the partners. Only the partner that is working at his or her coalface knows what is likely to happen in the next 12 months. The other key aspect of budgeting is that, as a result of creating budgets, it is also necessary to allocate responsibility for achieving the budget. If the partners are not involved in the setting of the budgets then it is highly unlikely that the partners will accept responsibility for their share of the budgets.

When setting budgets and breaking targets down to an individual level it is important to prepare tailored budgets which take into account the particular circumstances of individuals. Many firms have made the mistake of giving everybody at a certain level the same target. While this may in budgetary terms lead to a reasonable result, it is unlikely that these budgets will be motivational. For example, somebody who already beat the budget last year is hardly likely to be motivated by a budget at a lower level than was achieved and equally somebody who is currently performing way below the budget level may not be motivated by an average budget. While the overall budget is important, it is essential that detailed individual targets are set to try to improve the performance of each and every individual so that the performance of the firm as a whole is enhanced.

The second aspect of the financial cycle is the preparation and use of management information. Figure 5 suggests that management information should be distributed to managers. Prior to the development of information technology within firms there was often no information to be distributed and hence partners had to manage the practice by the seat of their pants. With the advent of information techology, there is often reams and reams of information made available to partners which they fail to use simply because of the volume of material that is provided to them. The aim must be to produce the right information to the right people so that effective management can take place.

Just who are the 'managers' in a law firm? A common problem in many firms is that people believe that all financial information should be confidential to the partnership. Indeed some firms treat all financial information as being so confidential that only certain equity partners are allowed to see it. In many cases, firms are getting confused. While it is right that certain financial information such as the profit shares of individual partners and maybe the profitability of the firm as a whole should only be disclosed to certain partners, there is no reason why other financial information should not be disclosed to all fee earners and that appropriate financial information should not be disclosed to people who are managing administrative functions. Without such information it is extremely hard for anybody to measure their effectiveness in performing their role. Fee earners who appreciate exactly how the business operates are likely to make a greater contribution. In a later chapter more detailed information is provided on the kind of information that might be provided to all fee earners, but at this stage it is important simply to understand that many firms have already recognised the importance of disclosing certain financial information to all fee earners to enable them to be both good solicitors and good business people.

The annual accounts that are produced in firms have been an annual source of amusement for many partners. As Figure 5 suggests, these accounts are normally produced for third parties such as the Inland Revenue and banks who rely on this annual information. Because the accounts have been prepared primarily for third parties, firms normally produce these accounts on the basis of limited disclosure since providing unnecessary information may lead to unnecessary questions from such third parties.

Annual budgets

Figure 6 provides a profit and loss account for a 4 partner firm. When talking to the partners in a firm such as this, the question that is at the top of everybody's agenda is, how can we increase the net profit of £200,000? This profit equates to a profit of just £50,000 per partner if there are 4 partners. Every partner will have read of far higher levels of profit being earned in other firms and will want to know how such profit can be achieved.

Figure 6   Example profit and loss account

	£
Fee income (4 partners)	1,000,000
Professional staff costs	450,000
Gross profit	550,000
Overheads	(350,000)
Equity partner profit	£200,000

From the material covered in Chapter 2 it is already possible to assess the profitability of this firm by looking at the net profit. Earning £200,000 on fee income of £1 million is a net profit percentage of only 20%. An efficient firm would be looking for a net profit percentage of 33% giving a net profit of £330,000 or just over £80,000 per partner. Why isn't the firm achieving a net profit percentage of 33%? One might have expected the overheads to be one third of fee income, i.e., about £333,000, so the amount being spent on overheads is only slightly above that. Professional staff costs should also have been one third of fee income or £333,000 so a cost figure of a further £117,000 is the major reason for lower profitability. The crucial action for this firm, therefore, is to try to achieve a higher level of fees from the existing professional staff costs or alternatively to reduce professional staff costs down to a more reasonable figure given the level of fee income being produced.

It is apparent from Figure 6 that, in preparing the budgets for the following year, the firm must produce a budget for fee income, a budget for professional staff costs and a budget for overheads because the budgeted profit will be the aggregation of these three budgets.

Fee income budget

Fee income is the largest figure in a profit and loss account and is the hardest figure to budget. Because of its size it is important that it is budgeted as accurately as possible and the following matters certainly need to be taken into consideration:

1   The charge-out rates used should be set to maximise gross profit and not fee income

When league tables are produced for firms they are normally ranked in terms of the size of fee income. Most partners would rather work for firms that achieved high profits than for firms that achieved high gross fees per partner. While there often is a correlation between the two figures there is not an immediate correlation in every case. Firms appreciate that it is necessary to increase fee income per partner to achieve higher profits. Often in an effort to increase fees there is little increase in additional profit because the work that is taken on is of a very low margin or, with larger fee portfolios, the overall efficiency of that portfolio decreases and while fee income has increased the level of profitability remains static or increases only marginally.

A new partner who, on becoming a partner, inherits a number of poor clients from fellow partners may well be advised to tinker with charge-out rates quite dramatically. It may be possible, for example, to sort out the good clients from the bad by doubling the fees charged to every client in the original list. The worst outcome of such an action is that a year later there may be no clients left, but it is more likely that there will still be a large number of clients left and an equivalent level of fee income will be earned in a much smaller amount of time, thus freeing up time for the new partner to go out and attract a higher quality of work for the future.

2   Split the budget between services/departments

The fee income budget must be analysed between the various departments within the firm and further analysis should perhaps be made within each department to reflect the different categories of work being undertaken.

3 Split the budget by month/quarter to allow for growth and seasonal variations

Fee income is not necessarily earned in twelve equal chunks throughout a year and there may be a certain degree of seasonality in the work that is undertaken and when bills can be delivered. This should be taken into account or else, in any one month when management information is prepared, people may take the wrong actions when comparing actual figures with budget figures. It is also important to take this into account in periods of growth. For example, if a partner had billed £240,000 last year and is budgeting for fees of £480,000 in the following year then, while that would equate to an average of £40,000 per month in the following year, it is highly unlikely that fees will be £40,000 per month. This is because if in aggregate fees are being doubled for the year as a whole, then fees will probably be around £25,000 per month at the start of the year and around £55,000 per month at the end of the year.

4 Take into account history, known future work and marketing activity

History is the best indicator of future performance. It is easy to produce an over ambitious fee income target which may well lead to the firm increasing its cost base. This could be extremely dangerous because although fee income may not be certain, once costs are incurred it may be difficult to back out of them. Relying on trends is therefore certainly a good way of assessing the achievability of budgets that are produced. Some partners are able to access, when budgeting, the amount of work that is already known. For example, sometimes by simply counting the number of files that are in progress it is possible to work out what the likely fee income is going to be from those files given the average fee that would be charged per file. Equally it may be possible, based on previous experience, to assess what further work can be generated through marketing activities. This is always going to be an imprecise calculation but when marketing has been undertaken over a number of years partners can become more certain that certain types of marketing will generate new work.

5 Prepare optimistic and pessimistic budgets

At the end of the budgeting process it is right to use a budget which represents the best guess of likely results. The preparation of optimistic and pessimistic budgets in addition will often be useful. An optimistic budget will make a partner feel happy and be a reminder that anything is in fact possible! Perhaps more importantly it is right to prepare a pessimistic budget which will show what might happen if things go wrong.

For example, what will happen if the new work that is anticipated doesn't arise and what will happen if the major client or clients choose to use another firm next year? If the outcome would be that the firm goes bankrupt then perhaps the whole budgeting process should start again because, while a firm is extremely unlikely to suffer an unlimited number of bad years, it is probably reckless to begin a year with a budget which could lead to the firm becoming insolvent if the firm is simply unlucky.

6 Ensure responsibility is allocated for the fee income budget

The main aim of the budgetary process is to ensure that there are sound budgets to manage the business. The preparation of the budgets alone is not sufficient and shares of the budgets must be allocated out to individual partners who must manage their share of the budget and accept responsibility for it.

7 Other income

Given that many firms are finding it increasingly difficult to maintain or increase fee income from traditional sources of business, it is always important when budgeting to look for alternative sources of income. For example, it may be possible to rent out surplus office space or to earn higher levels of interest through the use of client money. Other opportunities now also exist through the earning of financial services commissions, through fund management and through the provision of other non-traditional legal services.

Professional staff costs budget

When this budget is produced in a firm, the most common mistake is that nobody actually manages it. One often hears of firms where all of the partners know at the end of the year that they have all individually exceeded their fee income budgets and that they therefore expect to see a large profit figure only to have their hopes dashed when the accounts are finally produced. The reason why profits have not increased as much as they might have liked is because professional staff costs have increased just as quickly as fee income. When preparing this budget the following matters should be taken into account.

1 Analyse the cost into its constituent parts

While the primary cost is salaries it is probably right to include associated salary costs with this figure such as training, the provision of cars, pension costs or other benefits where applicable. It is important to set these figures out separately because when increases that may take place in the following year are looked at, the appropriate percentage increases may vary widely across the various types of cost.

2 Consider inflation carefully

When looking at how professional staff costs are going to increase from year to year it would be wrong to use the increase in the RPI index because inflation affects different costs in different ways. Just because the RPI index is increasing at 3% per annum does not mean that salaries will increase by 3% per annum and indeed it may be that the rate of increase in salaries will be different for fee earners as opposed to non-fee earning staff. Given the large size of this cost it is important to think very carefully about the inflationary element of this cost when budgeting or else there could be large variations materialising later in the year.

3 Efficiency variations through changes in staff structures

As clients become more cost conscious and force fees down for certain types of services, the only way that firms can hope to maintain levels of profitability is by reducing their cost base. To reduce the cost base may well mean changing the type of staff that are employed to provide these services to clients. For example, it may no longer be appropriate to employ highly paid assistant solicitors to do all of the work if some of the work can be done by lesser skilled and therefore lower paid people with the support of information technology etc.

4 Allocate responsibility for the budget

As stated in the introductory paragraph to this section it is important that somebody takes responsibility for this budget and manages the actual cost during the year against the budget and takes appropriate action. This is often overlooked and a small variance in this figure can have a large effect on overall profitability.

5 Make use of regional variations

Increasingly, medium and large sized firms are looking to provide a more cost effective service to clients by attracting work in areas where high fees can be charged and then undertaking the work in other areas where staff can be employed more cheaply and perhaps be accommodated in cheaper premises. For example, a firm that can attract work in London but which can successfully undertake the work in the Midlands or the North may be able to achieve significant cost savings compared with a firm that only employs staff in London. This issue does not just apply to the large national firms, it may be possible to have city centre premises which attract work at city centre rates with the majority of the staff being employed more cheaply out of the city centre in lower cost premises. This is becoming increasingly popular in offices that have made greater use of modern communication systems. There seems little doubt that working from home and hot desking will become increasingly important over the next few years.

Overheads budget

The following items need to be considered when preparing a budget for overheads.

1 Start with last year

While starting with a blank piece of paper may lead to a lower budget than in the previous year, it is not always that easy simply to eliminate overheads. Starting with last year will at least mean starting with a sense of reality.

2 Apply inflation appropriately

In the same way as was discussed for professional staff costs, inflation will affect different overheads in different ways. Some overheads will not increase in line with inflation, e.g., depreciation, which is based on historic cost, while other overheads will increase at varying rates.

3 Don't budget for 'general' or 'sundry' expenses

While some expenses might be categorised as sundry or general in the accounts that are produced during the year, it is usually wrong to budget under these headings. This is because it is extremely difficult to say who should approve any expenditure under these headings, so if anybody wants to sneak through an expense they simply call it sundries and there is less scrutiny. If you want to spend money on a certain area then budget for it, if you don't then don't have a budget heading for it and ensure that an appropriate person approves any additional expenditure during the year. When the accounts for professional firms are scrutinised, the one overhead category that is invariably overspent is general or sundry expenses because of this lack of control.

4   Consider having greater analysis of overheads than is provided in the annual accounts

Annual accounts provide a certain degree of analysis of overheads so that the reader of the accounts can see in some detail how expenses were incurred. From a management point of view it may be necessary throughout the year to have a more detailed analysis so that it is possible to identify precisely what action is required. For example, if a firm is worried because the expenditure on postage, packaging, stationery and photocopying has doubled since last year, it will not immediately know the cause of this increased cost. The only way that this could be determined is by analysing the heading out into its four constituent parts and seeing which part is the major share and which part has increased dramatically when compared with the previous year. Providing more detailed analysis of this type is easily done with most computer systems.

5   Considering the optimum level of expenditure

The question that many partners struggle with is deciding exactly what is the right amount to be spending on stationery or cleaning or insurance or couriers or any overhead within a particular year. It is extremely difficult when budgeting to decide for each overhead whether too much or too little is being spent even if you know in aggregate that you shouldn't be spending more than one third of your fee income on such costs. This is never going to be a precise science but one way of tackling such an exercise is to calculate each overhead as a percentage of gross fees and to do this for a number of years. Over a period of time, most overheads increase in line with fee income. For example, while rents may be fixed for the next few years they will eventually be reviewed and at such time larger premises may well be required in line with the increased fee income and so the percentage remains unchanged. More immediate changes are seen with costs such as telephone, stationery and secretarial staff costs when, with increasing volumes of work, this normally leads to a corresponding increase in the cost. Calculating each cost as a percentage of fee income over a number of years will therefore highlight any trends that may have happened and may help firms to identify those costs which are growing out of control and equally, perhaps, those areas where expenditure has been reduced too far.

6   Allocate responsibility

As with all other parts of the budget, it is important that overheads are managed throughout the year. This management is normally straightforward since with practice overheads can normally be budgeted extremely accurately and it is unlikely that there will be any significant variances. However, just because it is unlikely that there will be variances is no excuse for not managing the costs throughout the year.

7   Build in costs relating to longer term objectives

The master budget details what needs to happen over a 3–5 year period. Such plans will invariably involve incurring costs in the short term. It is important that such costs are built into the annual budget as otherwise the longer term goals may not be achieved.

What happens when the budgets have been set?

The three budgets discussed above are the most important parts of the budgeting process in a professional firm and determine the profit levels that are likely to be achieved. Having set these targets it is then necessary to produce a cash flow forecast for the current year that will determine the peaks and troughs in cash balances throughout the year and to produce a projected balance sheet at the end of the year to show how the net assets of the partnership will change. Although the preparation of a budgeted profit and loss account will provide an indication of the amount of profit that will be earned, it is impossible to determine the level of drawings that the partners can take until a cashflow forecast has been prepared for the year.

5

The Mechanics of Profitability — Gearing, Chargeable Hours, Charge-out Rates, Recovery and Margin

Partners are always interested in profitability but if the partners from one firm sat around a table and were asked what they should do to increase profitability they would normally come up with different answers. There will then often be some debate and indeed disagreement over what is the correct priority with regard to all of the suggestions that have been raised. A simpler way of understanding profitability and what can be done to improve financial performance can be gained through the use of a formula:

Average annual equity partner profit =

Gearing

×

Chargeable hours

×

Charge-out rate

×

Recovery

×

Margin

It is important to understand each of these terms and to understand the averages that exist within law firms so that an individual firm or a department within a firm can establish the variances that exist and hence the strengths and weaknesses of the firm or department.

Gearing

This is the average number of fee earners per equity partner. The way in which this affects profitability is really very straightforward. If a sole practitioner works on his own with no staff then the only profit that can be generated is the profit that is generated by the partner. Given that there are only 24 hours in a day, there is a limit to the amount of work that can be undertaken. If a sole practitioner is busy and work is still pouring in, then it makes sense to take on additional staff as employees whether they be assistant solicitors, legal executives or trainee solicitors to assist with professional work. Provided that each of these staff members can be charged out for more than it costs the solicitor to employ each staff member, the partner can then earn the self-generated profit together with the profit that is earned on each and every member of staff.

The more staff that are taken on, the bigger the pyramid becomes and the bigger the potential to earn higher levels of profit. It is important to realise, however, that this is not a one way street and while larger staff numbers can lead to larger profits, higher levels of gearing can work against the firm in that if nobody has enough work to do then everybody creates a loss for the firm.

Many solicitors believe that gearing is the primary factor that affects profitability and people often believe that the larger firms have very high levels of gearing compared with smaller firms and that this is the major difference between firms of different size. While the very largest London firms do have higher levels of gearing than average, many medium to large sized firms have similar levels of gearing to smaller firms. In many cases smaller firms are more highly geared than larger firms.

Chargeable hours

Fee earners are paid a salary for the services they perform and increasing chargeable hours by one hour, ten hours or one hundred hours has no immediate cost implications to the firm, the additional hours being potential pure profit. The figure that is used in the above formula is average chargeable hours per fee earner and it is important to ensure that all fee earners increase their hours and that a situation where one person increases chargeable hours but another fee earner decreases chargeable hours by a corresponding amount does not occur.

Charge-out rates

The figure used in the formula is the average charge-out rate per fee earner. As above, when discussing chargeable hours, fee earners are paid fixed salaries and if it is possible to increase the hourly charge-out rate this increase is pure profit as there would be no further cost implications.

When these first three factors are combined together, namely gearing, chargeable hours and charge-out rate we arrive at a figure which equates to work in progress. Work in progress printouts are simply a list of the people who have worked on a particular matter, the hours they have recorded and the charge-out rates that have been used.

Recovery

Recovery is the proportion of work in progress that has been billed. Figure 7 illustrates the calculation of recovery. If £10,000 has been recorded in the work in progress system but a final bill is issued for just £8,000 then there has been 80% recovery of time. In the same circumstances if a bill of £15,000 had been raised then there would have been 150% recovery because 150% of recorded time would have been billed. Small changes in recovery can have a very significant effect on profitability. If recovery changes by 1% this equates to fee income increasing from £100 to £101. If fee income goes up by 1% then net profits which on average are 25% would increase to 26% giving rise to a 4% increase in profits. In other words, a 10% increase in recovery would lead to a 40% increase in net profits, or a 5% increase in recovery would give rise to a 20% increase in net profits for an average firm.

Figure 7   Recovery

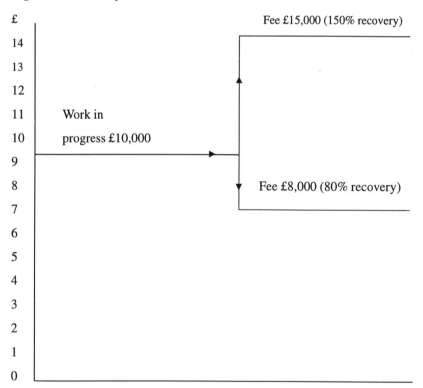

These four factors, namely gearing, chargeable hours, charge-out rates and recovery when combined together, give rise to gross fees per equity partner.

Margin

The formula is attempting to work out the net profit per equity partner and the first four factors have given the gross fees per equity partner. Gross fees is the figure at the top of the profit and loss account while net profit is the figure at the bottom of the profit and loss account. To get from the top to the bottom it is necessary to multiply by the margin. In other words, we now take account of all of the costs per equity partner that are going to be incurred by the firm. These costs will be all the professional staff costs and all the overheads.

Gearing, chargeable hours, charge-out rates, recovery and margin — who influences performance?

When considering each of these five factors it is important to recognise who can influence performance in each of them. In terms of the margin, or the costs that are to be involved, there is very little that partners or staff can do on a day-to-day basis once annual budgets have been established. For example, once a lease has been signed on the premises, little can be done to vary the premises costs and, equally, on support staff costs little variation will happen once the budget has been set at the start of the year. Other overheads may vary slightly against budget but there is unlikely to be that much flexibility during the year. The costs are therefore something which most people cannot affect dramatically throughout the year.

Of the remaining four factors, two can be dramatically influenced by all fee earners and two are probably more commonly under the control of the partners. The two that can be influenced by all fee earners are chargeable hours and recovery and these are probably the two factors which have the greatest effect on profitability. This is good news because it means that firms can involve fee earners in increasing the profitability of the firm. Equally it could be bad news because if fee earners choose not to perform to the best of their abilities this will have a dramatic adverse effect on the profitability of that firm.

Gearing and charge-out rates can be influenced by all fee earners in the firm but these factors tend to be controlled by the partners.

It is worth noting that in many cases there is a link between these factors and they should not be looked at in isolation. For example, increasing gearing normally also increases chargeable hours because any administration is spread over a larger number of people. Increased gearing usually reduces average charge-out rates as gearing is normally increased with the addition of junior fee earners.

The rest of this chapter is devoted to looking at industry averages for gearing, chargeable hours, charge-out rates and recovery and presents some ideas on how firms can improve their current levels of performance.

Industry averages for gearing

Figure 8 provides some information on how a typical firm will be structured in terms of types of partner and employee. There will be differences from firm to firm and from department to department within a firm but it is still always worth starting by comparing the existing staff structure of a firm or department with some average figures.

Figure 8   Typical staff structures

	%
Equity partners	11
Salaried partners	4
Assistant solicitors	16
Legal executives & paralegals	7
Trainees	7
Total fee earners	45
Secretaries	35
Accounts/cashiers	6
Other administration	14
Total staff	100

On reviewing Figure 8 the first thing that becomes apparent to most partners is the split of fee earning and non-fee earning staff. Fifty five per cent of staff members are non-fee earning, being secretaries 35%, accounts/cashiers 6%, other administration 14%. Perhaps the key ratio that firms need to look at is the ratio of secretaries to fee earners and in Figure 8 this would be 35 secretaries to 45 fee earners or, put more simply, 7 secretaries for every 9 fee earners. There is a growing trend in law firms to try to change this ratio and a common target is to get to a position where there is 1 secretary for every 2 fee earners. This is unlikely to be achievable over a short period of time and may well be one of the aims for a firm over a 3–5 year period. There is little doubt that such change is achievable, particularly with the development of information technology within firms. Now that so many documents are held on the system and can be amended quickly rather than being retyped this should lead to efficiencies. Also, the fact that more fee earners have terminals on their desks should mean that they are able to put through minor amendments for themselves in a more efficient way than relying on secretaries. Such a change requires a change of culture within the firm and this is why the process is likely to be gradual rather than immediate. The knock-on effect of such change is that secretaries will in many cases cease to become word-processor operators and take on a more traditional secretarial role for partners which may ultimately result in them becoming partially chargeable through the work that they undertake.

Turning to the 45% of staff who are fee earners, the first ratio that may be calculated is the gearing ratio. With these figures there are 2 fee earners for every partner or if one simply looks at equity partners there are 3 fee earners for every equity partner. Pyramids are therefore not normally that large although in some larger firms the gearing per equity partner gets as high as 8 or 9 fee earners per equity partner. Some very small firms achieve even higher levels of gearing with figures as high as 40 fee earners per equity partner being observed.

The most numerous fee earners are the assistant solicitors. In recent years there has been a growing trend in the use of other fee earners such as legal executives and paralegals and in many surveys of professional firms one sees on a year by year basis a gradual shift in this direction. This would appear to be a trend that will continue since clients are now demanding lower fees for certain types of work and this can only be achieved if firms are willing to reduce the cost base associated with such work.

An increasing number of firms have been questioning in recent years whether they should continue to train solicitors. The benefit is probably a medium to long term benefit in that high quality qualified staff will be developed if they are trained within the firm. The alternative is not to train but to bring in qualified staff from other firms, but then there is the disadvantage that people have been trained in a different culture and a different environment and such people may take some time to fit in to a new firm.

A useful exercise for any firm is to take the telephone list and analyse it in line with Figure 8 to see how the firm differs from the averages. A variance from the average does not necessarily mean a particular firm is doing better or worse because there can be logical grounds for variations to an average structure. It is important for firms to identify the preferred staff structures which are required so that, over a period of 1–3 years, adjustments can be made to the staff structure in a disciplined way rather than always taking short term reactions to replace staff turnover. Many firms have no proper manpower plan. Whenever someone leaves the immediate reaction is to fill the vacancy rather than considering whether this change is part of a longer term plan. Individual firms must make sure that they are competitive with their immediate rivals rather than just with the profession in general.

Industry averages for chargeable hours

Figure 9 provides an indication of the average chargeable hours that are recorded in firms together with an indication of the common highs and lows that are observed in interfirm comparisons.

Figure 9   Average chargeable hours

	High	Average	Low
Partners	1,400	1,150	800
Assistants	1,750	1,200	700
Legal executives & paralegals	1,550	1,100	650
Trainees	1,450	950	750

Starting with partners, what level of chargeable hours should be recorded on an annual basis? Perhaps the most common figure seen is somewhere between 1,150 and 1,200 hours per annum, with a range from 800 to 1,400 hours per annum. This equates to an average of approximately 100 hours per month or 25 hours per week assuming people work throughout the year. If a partner comes from a firm where an average level of chargeable hours is being recorded, there is often a great temptation to try to increase hours to a level where partners are recording a higher level of chargeable hours, such as 1,350 hours per annum. An increase from 1,150 to 1,350 hours per annum is a further 200 chargeable hours per year. To achieve this would involve a further 4 hours of chargeable time a week or an increase of approximately 50 minutes per day. If a partner charges his time at £100 an hour this would result in a further £20,000 of chargeable time being created and therefore many partners immediately say they will achieve this increase because of the further £20,000 of profit that will be created. This would be a grave mistake potentially in many firms and is best understood by considering the position of assistant solicitors.

One would expect the chargeable hours recorded by assistant solicitors to be considerably higher than the figure recorded by partners. This should be the case because normally assistant solicitors are not expected to spend as much time on marketing, client development and administration matters. How many more hours this is going to amount to will vary from individual to individual but one might have expected a further 15% to 20% of time to be recorded, giving a figure of approximately 1,400 chargeable hours per annum. In practice, as Figure 9 shows, the average for assistant solicitors is only 50 hours more per year than for partners or 1 hour a week or 12 minutes a day. While this is surprising, it is worth noting the range that exists at the assistant solicitor level and the figure shows a range of 700 to 1,750 hours per annum being recorded.

The greatest influence on profitability within professional firms as observed in interfirm comparisons is the chargeable hours of assistant solicitors. There is normally an immediate correlation in surveys with the firm which achieves the highest chargeable hours per assistant solicitor achieving the highest profit levels per partner. This is easily understood if one considers the change that will happen in moving from recording an average number of hours for an assistant solicitor of 1,200 per annum up to a high performing firm at 1,700 hours per annum. If on average there are 3 fee earners working for each equity partner and these are mainly assistants then as far as each equity partner is concerned there are a further 1,500 hours created. If a rate of £66 per hour was used this would equate to an increase in profits of £100,000 per partner. Far higher increases in profits can be achieved than by partners simply capturing more chargeable time for themselves. The rule of thumb that many firms could follow therefore is to aim for partners to achieve an average number of chargeable hours but for assistants to record a high number of chargeable hours. This will only be possible in firms where partners protect enough time for marketing and for managing staff so that assistant solicitors are able to perform at these higher levels.

The figure for paralegals and legal executives are similar to those for assistant solicitors but are normally a little lower. There is no obvious reason for this other than perhaps that they often have a more limited career structure than assistant solicitors and therefore do not always put in the extra hours that assistant solicitors do to advance their careers.

The figure for trainee solicitors is somewhat lower and this is probably in line with expectations, given the training that takes place.

The model for firms to follow that want to achieve higher levels of profitability is to go for average hours for partners, high hours for assistant solicitors, paralegals and legal executives and average or low hours for trainee solicitors. A firm that boasts that it has the highest chargeable hours figure for trainee solicitors is unlikely to be highly profitable because to achieve this result it is probably necessary for more expensive fee earners to run around and to waste time to keep the trainees busy. It is unlikely that any firm could achieve the high figures for every category and therefore the sort of model that is being suggested is a more realistic target.

An issue that is often raised when discussing chargeable time is, how on earth do some firms manage to obtain 1,750 chargeable hours from assistant solicitors? There is a common belief that assistant solicitors who achieve this level of chargeable time will have a lower life expectancy and higher divorce rate than usual but this is not necessarily the case.

Figure 10 shows how a typical partner allocates time throughout a year and Figure 11 provides a similar calculation for a typical assistant solicitor. Figure 10 illustrates quite clearly that it is possible to increase chargeable time from 1,150 to 1,350 chargeable hours without working any longer days, if one simply captures some of the lost time which never appears on time sheets but is actually worked. Figure 11 is even more alarming in that there is even more lost time and an even greater potential to increase chargeable time. For assistant solicitors it is possible to get to a chargeable hours figure of 1,750 hours per annum without working any longer hours than the hours that are currently being worked. It is simply a case of recording chargeable time as such.

Figure 10   How the year is spent — partners

Annual hours (7 ½ per day × 5 days × 52 weeks)			1,950
Less: Holidays	300		
Sickness	35		
Training	35		
	___		
			(370)
			‾‾‾‾‾
			1,580
Less: Marketing	5		
Admin	5		
	___		
	10	× 42 in office	(420)
			1,160
Actual chargeable hours (per Figure 9)			(1,150)
'Wasted' hours			10
Additional hours worked 42 × 10			420
'Missing' time each year			430
			‾‾‾‾‾

Figure 11   How time is spent — Assistants

Annual hours (7 ½ per day × 5 days × 52 weeks)			1,950
Additional hours worked (1 per day × 5 × 44 weeks)			220
			‾‾‾‾‾
			2,170
Less: Holidays	225		
Sickness	35		
Training	35		
	___		
			(295)
			‾‾‾‾‾
			1,875
Actual chargeable hours (per Figure 9)			(1,200)
'Missing' time each year			675
			‾‾‾‾‾

Increasing chargeable hours at any level will only happen if partners give clear instructions to fee earners as to how they expect time to be recorded. In many firms there is great inconsistency between fee earners with regard to time recording and firms need greater clarity. The following situations highlight some of the common inconsistencies that arise:

(a)   During a typical day in the office you consider that you have spent 30 minutes making trips to the toilet, the coffee machine and making a personal call.

(b)   Same facts as (a) but you worked all day on one client at their premises.

(c)   While in the office, somebody comes and talks to you on a non-client matter for 15 minutes.

(d)   A client telephones you for some advice which is helpful — the call lasts just 3 minutes.

(e)   Same facts as (d) but the call lasts 15 minutes.

(f)   You go to lunch with a client and talk primarily about the client's business; the lunch lasts 90 minutes.

(g)   Same facts as (f) but lunch takes an hour.

(h)   Same facts as (f) but lunch takes two hours.

(i)   You research a technical point for a client and this takes 30 minutes.

(j)   Same facts as (i) but you feel you should have known the answer.

(k)   Same facts as (i) but you think another person might have taken 2 hours to do the research.

(l)   Same facts as (i), another client asks you the same question and you can reply immediately in 2 minutes.

(m)   Getting to work normally takes 45 minutes but getting to this particular client takes 75 minutes.

(n)   During lunch you discuss a technical point with a colleague, this saves you an hour of research.

(o)   You review a file at home, the night before seeing a client and this takes 3 hours.

Without some rules being established that deal with the above questions it is likely that a considerable amount of chargeable time will go 'missing' each year. Such time will either not appear on time sheets or will appear under a non-chargeable code. 'Missing' time is most likely to be an issue at the lower end of the hierarchy as such fee earners usually have lower confidence when it comes to recording chargeable time as such.

The above questions can be used for setting standards for time recording that should encourage people, particularly those more junior in the hierarchy, to record chargeable time as such.

Another technique that partners and senior fee earners can adopt is to ask members of staff to account for their time at the end of each day. Typically on such a review, it is discovered that only 7 ½ hours of time have been recorded on the time sheet despite the fact that the employee has been in the office for perhaps 10 ½ hours. On discussion, it transpires that one of these hours was a lunch hour but that two hours of time spent in the office had not been recorded on a time sheet. When pushed, the fee earner will account for the other two hours and will probably account for these as more non-chargeable time. Any time which has already been recorded as non-chargeable and this further time that has now been allocated as such, could be discussed in more detail and perhaps small amounts of this time can be shifted into the chargeable category. Only a very small shift of half an hour to an hour a day needs to be achieved to have an extremely significant effect on profitability.

Such a procedure may be effective for a period of about a week in increasing the level of chargeable time but it is not right to carry on with this procedure indefinitely. There is a danger, however, that once the procedure has stopped, fee earners will slip back into bad habits and that chargeable time will start to reduce but the procedure could be repeated on a regular basis, perhaps every six months.

Later in this chapter, the effect on billing of recording more chargeable time will be considered, but at this stage we are simply looking at how fee earners can be encouraged to record all chargeable time as such.

Industry averages for charge-out rates

Figure 12 indicates average rates for medium to large sized London firms and gives some idea of the sort of range that might exist for such firms. Clearly, these rates will not be common across all London firms and there will be significant variances across the country.

Figure 12   Charge-out rates — medium to large London firms

	£ per hour
Partners	240
3–4 year qualified assistants	160
Non-solicitors	90
Trainees	75
	£565

It is interesting to stop and consider the methods that are used in setting charge-out rates within firms. Historically, the major driving force has been the expense of time calculation. To perform this calculation, the firm has to look at all of its costs, both fixed and variable, and add an element of profit to these costs to arrive at a total figure which must be charged out by fee earners. The allocation between fee earners is made on the basis of a certain number of chargeable hours being recorded by each type of fee earner and, having allocated out these hours, a rate is then used for each fee earner which will lead to the correct total amount of chargeable time being recorded. The differentials between rates using this method are linked to the cost of each person. While in general terms, as people progress, their salaries increase and their ability to charge higher hourly rates increases, there is not a strict correlation between the cost of an employee and the charge-out rate that can be applied. In particular, there are certain points during a fee earner's career when salary levels are perhaps hiked up too quickly and it is not possible to pass on this additional cost to clients immediately.

Recently, the driving force for charge-out rates has become the importance of following the flock. In other words, firms are now setting their charge-out rates based on what other firms are doing and are paying less attention to expense of time calculations. It is no longer possible simply to set rates at the required level to earn a certain level of profit. If everybody else has restructured and is able to provide the same service at a lower rate then there is no choice but to reduce rates. Differentials between firms in terms of charge-out rates have become most marked in recent times and in particular there is often a significant difference between the rates charged by larger London firms and those which are charged by provincial firms.

What are firms trying to achieve by setting charge-out rates at different levels for individual employees? The obvious answer is that charge-out rates should be set to encourage delegation to the optimum level. In other words, partners and senior fee earners should not be hanging on to work simply to meet their own personal chargeable hour targets but they should be delegating work to people who are able to undertake the work in a more cost effective way. This clearly does not happen in many firms and all too often one is aware of the ''smine' concept prevailing. This is the concept whereby once a file has landed on someone's desk, they hang on to it and say ''smine' because this helps with a personal target.

On reviewing Figure 12 it is easy to ask whether or not the differentials are adequate between the levels indicated to encourage delegation in all cases. It is possible to set charge-out rates with a greater range between the top and bottom of the hierarchy as indicated in Figure 13.

Figure 13   Charge-out rates — medium to large London firms
Alternative rates

	£ per hour
Partners	270
3–4 year qualified assistants	165
Non-solicitors	80
Trainees	50
	£565

There is still the same total figure being recovered per hour assuming one person at each of the levels but there is now a greater range of rates. The benefit of such a scheme is that people towards the bottom of the hierarchy will appear cheaper and hence more senior fee earners are more likely to delegate work to them. Unless work is delegated, these junior people will remain less effective for longer because they will lack experience. The sooner that junior people have the skills necessary to undertake certain types of work the better, because then the firms can undercut their competitors who are unable to delegate this type of work.

There is a disadvantage in setting rates in this way and that is that if, in total, one is going to charge the same amount per hour, then partners and senior fee earners may need to have higher charge-out rates than those set by competing firms. While the headline partner rate is clearly extremely important, it need not be an insurmountable burden provided that these people genuinely appreciate that their rates are likely to be more than those in competing firms. In such a firm, if a partner goes out to pitch for some work, then provided the partner is happy to explain to the client that the partner rate is higher than that charged by competitors but that the partner proposes to delegate the work to people at much lower rates so that the overall cost will be lower, then there is no reason why the client will not offer the contract to this firm.

Another area that requires particular attention when considering charge-out rates are the rates that are allocated to individual partners within a firm. If the average rate for a partner in a particular firm was £170 per hour then the spread of rates around this is not normally that significant. The range may be from £150 to £190 and normally the lower rates will be allocated to the more junior partners and the higher rates to the more senior partners. It may be more appropriate to try and set rates which reflect the value that is being provided to clients and this may lead to a far wider range of rates being used. For example, a tax partner who doesn't generate any work directly but who provides high value advice on every transaction may be able to charge a significant premium on the usual rate. Often, politics within the firm prevent this from happening since it is assumed that only senior partners can have higher rates and that junior partners should always have lower rates.

Another example that helps to explain the problem with partner rates is to consider a new partner and a partner with approximately 15 years' experience and a mature client base. If the new partner was asked to generate 1,200 chargeable hours at a charge-out rate of £170 an hour as was the partner with considerable experience, then perhaps neither would have an adequate level of motivation. For the partner with considerable experience, such targets may be relatively easy and may mean just sitting back and waiting to achieve the target. For the new partner to achieve this level of hours or this level of charge-out rate may be almost impossible due to the lack of experience of the particular partner and the relative size and maturity of the existing client base. It may be better to set the new partner a lower rate and the more experienced partner a combination of rates which reflect the type of work undertaken. For example, the more experienced partner may be asked to do 1,000 hours at £170 an hour and the remaining 200 chargeable hours at a rate which is considerably higher, perhaps £250 per hour. If these hours at a higher rate could be achieved, then a further £16,000 of chargeable time would be created which would not only be of positive benefit to the firm but, more importantly, the partner would identify the types of services provided which are of high value to clients. Providing this sort of advice normally gives greater satisfaction to the partner and once such advice has been identified, the partner should then be motivated to provide more of this service to existing clients. More importantly, the 'ordinary' work of £170 an hour probably should be delegated to other partners or to senior fee earners. This process is likely to bring this to the attention of the partner faster and encourage the delegation that really should have started earlier.

Industry averages for recovery

Figure 14 indicates what usually happens when a fee earner comes to bill. Whatever the level of work in progress that has been created, it normally seems too much and as a consequence the fee earner ends up writing off a proportion of this work in progress before delivering a bill for the net amount. Recovery is the percentage of the work in progress that is billed, so the recovery in Figure 14 is 80%, but if a bill of £15,000 had been raised then recovery would have been 150%.

Figure 14   Recovery — normal pattern

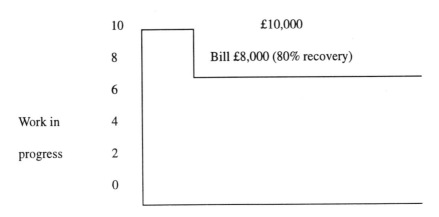

Most fee earners are not aware of the average recovery level across a period of time and simply remember the extremes and relate to this as the normal position. All fee earners can remember times when they were able to mark up bills dramatically and equally can probably remember times when a matter was completed yet it was impossible to raise any bill on the client. While these extremes provide lessons for the future, it is the overall average which has the greatest meaning at the end of each year.

Throughout this chapter, it has been suggested that firms should look to increase chargeable hours or charge-out rates as ways of increasing profitability. The obvious point that could be raised is that both of these suggestions are a waste of time since if extra time is recorded in the work in progress system, either as chargeable hours or an increase to the charge-out rate, then this increment will simply be written off at the time of billing and will lead to a reduction in recovery levels.

Figure 15 considers what would happen if the same matter as in Figure 14 was being handled again but on this occasion the fee earner recorded all chargeable time as such, or looked to record time at a high charge-out rate, or a combination of both.

Figure 15   Recovery — alternative approach

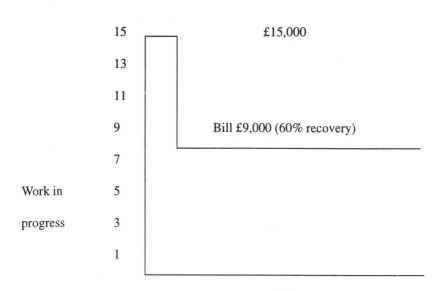

At the time of billing, the fee earner may have a mini crisis but psychologically would still try to recover as much of the time as possible and, although the recovery rate falls in the example to just 60%, the fee becomes £1,000 higher. At the end of the day, it is the fee that matters and this extra £1,000 of fee is pure profit. For a typical firm making 25% net profit, an extra £1,000 on an £8,000 fee is 12 ½% more fee income but this would lead to a further 50% in net profit. Most fee earners are blissfully unaware of the significance of recovery on profitability.

If a bill of £1,000 is about to be issued then more junior fee earners are unlikely to encourage the partner to increase the bill to, say, £1,010, being an increase of 1%. To argue over a 1% increase may seem ridiculous but given that this would on average lead to a 4% increase in profits it is actually quite significant. To increase the bill to £1,050, a 5% increase to the bill, would lead to an average increase in profits of 20%. Billing is about confidence and it is always easy to underbill because of the fear that a client will object to paying the bill or that perhaps the client will go elsewhere next time. While fees are an issue, it is unlikely that clients will go through the aggravation of moving from one firm to another simply because a fee was a few percentage points higher than might have been expected, provided that the service that was being provided was of the highest quality.

Is this approach going to help on fixed fee situations? Suppose, looking at Figures 14 and 15, that a fixed fee had been quoted of £8,000. If the approach in Figure 14 had been adopted then with only £10,000 of work in progress it would not have been too difficult simply to write off £2,000 and issue a bill for £8,000. If, however, Figure 15 had been used, then with a fixed fee of £8,000 but work in progress of £15,000, a lot more effort would have gone into finding a way of increasing the bill. For example, it may have been possible to identify some extra work that was done over and above the fixed fee quoted. Even if it is impossible to increase the fee then a fee earner is unlikely to accept readily another instruction of the same sort once it is appreciated that £7,000 has been written off on the matter rather than just £2,000. The final reason why even under a fixed fee situation it is preferable to record time honestly is that it is better to tell a client that you have had to write off £7,000 rather than only £2,000.

There is a huge range of recovery rates being achieved by individual fee earners. There is a narrower range of recovery rates being achieved by individual departments and there is a narrower still range of recovery rates between firms.

Very few firms above ten partners in size can ever hope to recover more than 100% of their work in progress unless they operate a niche practice. Prior to the recession, extremely good performance for a firm of 10 or more partners would have been 95% recovery, but during the recession best performance has probably fallen back to around 92%. Average recovery rates in firms would typically be of the order of 85% and this means that some firms are recovering considerably less than 80% of time recorded.

An interesting question to ask in any firm is, what has happened to your recovery rate over the last 5 years and what has happened to your recorded chargeable hours and charge-out rates during this period? In many firms, the chargeable hours figure is effectively institutionalised and remains constant over each of these 5 years. Figure 16 illustrates what happens to the other two variables, i.e., charge-out rates and recovery.

Figure 16   Charge-out rates and recovery

Years ago	% Increase in charge-out rate	Recovery %
5	10	90
4	30	90
3	—	90
2	5	90
1	25	90

Charge-out rates in firms are not normally increased in equal amounts. There are rapid increases and then much smaller increases as the figure indicates. One might expect that in a year of rapid or high rate increases the recovery percentage would drop but that in years of little or no charge-out rate increase the recovery rate would increase. However, as the figure indicates, whatever the increase in charge-out rate, the recovery rate usually remains remarkably constant. It would appear that in most law firms the recovery rate is also institutionalised and that fee earners know the level of work in progress which can be written off without a lot of questions being asked. Because of this fact it should now be evident why it is important for firms either to increase charge-out rates or chargeable hours because it is highly unlikely that the extra work in progress that is created will all be written off.

Recovery is almost the hidden factor in profitability because it is not something that ever appears in a normal profit and loss account. The profit and loss account starts with fee income which is after recovery has been taken into account. To highlight the true cost of recovery and its effect on profitability, it may be useful for firms to create a profit and loss account as in Figure 17 because then recovery becomes a figure with real and visible value to all of the partners.

Figure 17   Alternative profit and loss account

	£
Chargeable time created in month	100,000
Less: time written off	(10,000)
	90,000
(Increase)/decrease in work in progress	(10,000)
Fee income	80,000
Less: professional staff costs	(30,000)
Gross profit	50,000
Overheads	(30,000)
Net profit	£20,000

Margin

The four factors that have already been considered in this chapter lead to fee income yet the chapter is trying to establish the level of profit that is earned by each equity partner. This final factor called 'margin' therefore takes all of the costs into account. There is very little that any fee earner can do to control costs on a day-to-day basis and therefore it is largely irrelevant. This does not mean that the costs themselves are irrelevant, simply that there is little that fee earners can do to reduce these costs in a material way.

The budgeting and the control of costs is left to managing or departmental managing partners and is an important exercise for these people.

6

Working Capital Control

A major and recurring problem in all professional firms is working capital control. Partners only have a finite amount of capital which they are able to introduce into the firm and this capital needs to be managed carefully or else sufficient capital may not be available to finance the practice. Many partnerships try never to borrow money while others have at some stage stumbled into borrowings and have never managed to get back to a cash position. Ending up with bank borrowings is almost inevitable for firms that expand if all profits are distributed and no profits are retained within the partnership to finance the expansion.

The primary reason why borrowings become necessary is because, while cash payments that are associated with running costs such as premises and staff costs go out on a regular basis, normally within a month from the time at which the cost is incurred, income raised through professional fees may not appear as cash for many months after the original instruction. The aspects of working capital that fee earners therefore need to manage in a professional firm are the control of work in progress and debtors.

As has already been stated above, from the moment an instruction is received, costs start to be incurred but it is often many months before a bill is issued and it may then be several months again before cash is finally received. The danger is that even though a practice is making profits, it will cease to trade because of the lack of cash and the inability to borrow further funds. Firms must therefore try to reduce as much as possible the delay between the receiving of an instruction and the date on which cash is finally received.

There will clearly be large differences in this regard between firms, between departments and between fee earners. Some of the differences are immediately understandable because of the nature of the work or the type of clients that are being serviced but other differences have no immediate explanation other than that one particular fee earner is better at managing this process than another fee earner.

Most firms are broadly aware of the importance of managing work in progress and debtors but rather than managing the complete time between the receipt of an instruction and the receipt of cash, firms often put overemphasis on one of the two parts of the process, i.e., either trying to accelerate the speed with which bills are issued, or trying to accelerate the cash collection period once the bill has been issued. If, for example, a firm tries to speed up the cash collection period, this may have no overall effect if fee earners simply delay issuing a bill until such a time as they feel confident that the client will be able to pay quickly.

Figure 18 illustrates the consequences of poor working capital control and the consequent problems that can arise with bank borrowings.

Figure 18   Poor working capital control

Profit and Loss Account

	£ million
Fee income	40
	==
Profit before interest	12
Interest	(3)
Net profit	£9
	==

Balance Sheet

Fixed assets	2
Debtors and work in progress	40
Creditors	(9)
Overdraft/borrowings	(27)
Net assets	£6
	==
Partners' capital	£6
	==

Figure 19 shows the same firm's balance sheet if there had been better working capital control and also shows the effect on profitability if such control was effected.

Figure 19   Typical working capital control

Profit and Loss Account

	£ million
Fee income	40
	==
Profit before interest	12
Interest	–
Profit after interest	£12
	==

Balance Sheet

	£ million
Fixed assets	2
Debtors and work in progress	15
Creditors	(9)
Overdraft	(2)
Net assets	£6
Partners' capital	£6

The majority of fee earners do not appreciate the effect on profitability of such control and also very few fee earners have any idea at all of the time scales involved between receiving an instruction and obtaining cash. Indeed, most fee earners think this total process is normally only three to four months. Figure 20 illustrates the range of time scales that are often seen with regard to working capital control.

Figure 20   Working capital control — debtor and work in progress days

	Work in progress Days	Debtors Days	Total credit given — days
Very good performance	90	75	165
Average performance	120	90	210
Very poor performance	360	180	540

Average performance involves providing clients with credit of approximately 210 days or 7 months. For a firm with fees of £12 million per annum, this equates to £7 million of credit. Reducing the period down from 210 days to 180 days would release £1 million of cash into the balance sheet. This extra cash makes the partnership more solvent but also means that the partnership potentially has free cash or bank facilities available which will enable the partnership to take on new opportunities when they arise.

In chapter 4, it was explained that one of the dangerous times for a professional firm is in a period of expansion following a recession. The problem that might arise is that while new work may seem very attractive, the firm may get into financial trouble simply because it has insufficient capital to finance the new work it has taken on. It is therefore extremely important that firms review new work carefully before accepting instructions: if clients take more credit than is expected, this can lead to additional financial problems for the firm.

Working Capital Control

Many firms do not account for work in progress at full value in the accounts and so there is no real figure in the accounts which demonstrates the amount of work in progress outstanding. Many firms will tell you that they are delighted to have high work in progress because they are delaying tax and they have fees in the cupboard for future years. While this may be the case, the firm would be considerably stronger if it had already billed and collected the cash and now had money in the bank earning interest.

In addition to controlling work in progress and debtors, firms must also measure the amount of unbilled disbursements. This can be measured in the same way as work in progress and debtors but the figures involved are normally considerably smaller and less significant.

Firms that wish to calculate the amount of credit that has been given to clients through work in progress and debtors must perform calculations on a regular basis to determine the figures. The formula for work in progress days, being the time between doing an hour of work and issuing a bill for that work, is:

$$\frac{\text{work in progress at month end}}{\text{inputs into work in progress over last year}} \times 365$$

The resultant figure from the calculation is a number of days' work in progress outstanding and shows the credit period that is being given before a bill is issued.

A similar calculation can be calculated for debtors which is called debtors days and this is:

$$\frac{\text{debtors excluding VAT}}{\text{fee issued in last year}} \times 365$$

The sum of these two periods is the total amount of credit that has been given to clients.

Firms that are poor at working capital control often believe that it will take them many years to improve their performance and bring them back in line with average firms or even to achieve above average performance. This belief centres around the fact that they feel it will be very difficult to re-educate existing clients to accept earlier bills and faster settlement. This fear is usually unfounded since, if fee earners move to other firms who only allow lower credit periods to clients, then clients normally immediately accept the new credit terms from the new firm provided that they are happy with the service that has been provided by the fee earners.

It is one thing to understand the mechanics of working capital control, it is another thing to achieve a reduction in the work in progress and debtors days figures when they are calculated. To reduce work in progress days requires a conscious effort from each fee earner and the use of interim bills and more regular billing will certainly help. From a management point of view, perhaps the most effective way of reducing this figure is to give each fee earner a target and to provide regular information on performance against this target. Management information and targets will probably also assist with debtors days but additional procedures such as the appointment of a credit controller or regular credit control meetings may also assist. Some firms introduce a formula whereby a partner's drawings will be limited unless work in progress and debtor control is achieved to a certain level.

7

Investment Appraisal

As was discussed in Chapter 6, firms only have a finite amount of capital to finance the firm. This capital comes either from the partners or from banks who are willing to advance funds.

Given that funds are usually tight and that any excess funds are normally needed to cover drawings, it is usually extremely difficult for firms to have a coherent investment policy. Possible new investments can vary tremendously from simply expanding an existing department through to establishing a new department within the office or opening a new office in another town or, in some cases, overseas.

In most firms, there will be plenty of investment opportunities. It is important that partners apply consistent financial criteria to measure the risks and rewards of all of the projects that are presented. Most partners can remember horrific investments that cost considerable sums of money which, in hindsight, they realise should never have been made but which at the time appeared to be exceptional opportunities.

Before considering any new opportunity, it is perhaps worth considering whether it will increase or decrease the partners' overall return on capital. An existing return on capital employed for most firms can sensibly be calculated as the profit before tax divided by partners capital. If capital is limited than it is important for any firm to maximise the return on this capital to as high a level as possible. While return on capital deposited in banks or building societies may only have been around 10% per annum in the last decade and in UK equities around 15% per annum over that period, professional firms have historically been able to earn at least 100% per annum on capital. If more capital is available then reasonable returns may also be possible but normally these very high rates of return are only associated with professional firms that carry high professional indemnity risks associated with the advice that is being given.

There are many ways of assessing new investments but perhaps the two most common methods used are payback and discounted cashflow techniques.

The payback method works on the basis of seeing how long it will be before the initial outlay of funds is recovered and the firm is back to a neutral position. In this day and age it is highly unlikely that a firm would like to undertake a new investment where the original capital outlay will not be recovered in a relatively short period of perhaps three to five years. The problem with only accepting projects that have a very short payback is that the longer term projects which could have a lasting and sustained effect on the firm are not accepted because of the additional payback risk. It may appear to be a rather pessimistic outlook to review investment projects simply on the speed with which original funds will be recouped but given that until such funds are recouped the practice could suffer a capital loss, it is always a worthwhile calculation.

The alternative and slightly more mathematically complicated approach is to look at discounted cashflows. An investment made today will yield returns in future years and then over a number of years the profitability of the project can be assessed. However, as Figure 21 shows, the value of the cashflows which are received in future years are not worth as much as the initial outlay today in pound terms because the value of a pound in a year's time is not worth as much as the value of a pound today.

Figure 21   Investment appraisal

Time	Detail	Cashflow £	Discount	Net present value
Now	Open new office	(150,000)	1	(150,000)
1 Year	Trading profit	70,000	$1/1.1$	63,636
2 Years	Trading profit	70,000	$1/1.1^2$	57,851
3 Years	Trading profit	70,000	$1/1.1^3$	52,592
4 Years	Trading profit	70,000	$1/1.1^4$	47,811
4 Years	Close office	(20,000)	$1/1.1^4$	(13,660)
		£110,000		£58,230

The future cashflows can be discounted using different rates. In some circumstances it may be appropriate to discount using the marginal cost of borrowing the funds that are used to finance the investment or, alternatively, it may be right to discount the cashflows using the existing return on capital employed to see whether or not this proposed new investment generates a higher or lower rate of return than the existing activities that are undertaken.

As a result of these investment criteria, it may well be that in many instances an investment opportunity will be turned down rather than accepted. If a firm is faced with two alternatives then often one of these is accepted rather than both being rejected.

Many firms still have rules within partnership agreements that require a higher percentage of partners to agree to an investment decision than are required for other decisions within the partnership. Such a rule may make partnerships more risk averse but at the same time such rules may protect them from crazy investments.

8

Management Reporting

It has already been established in chapter 4 that it is important for management information to be produced and for it to be disseminated to all fee earners who are managing client relationships. Many firms still fail to produce and disclose financial information to a large number of people who are carrying out management functions. The cloak of secrecy that surrounds partnership accounts has in many cases got out of hand and whenever information is produced that contains numbers partners automatically think that this information must be confidential. Clearly this is not always the case and while some information would be confidential to the partnership other financial information will be invaluable to fee earners in undertaking their fee earning responsibilities.

It is all a question of giving the right information to the right people. The managing partner of a firm needs to be provided with information on the firm as a whole since this is what he or she is managing. Such information will enable the managing partner to focus attention on the areas of the firm that require attention. When a firm is split into a number of departments, the partner who is responsible for running each of the departments within the firm should receive information on this department because that is the part of the firm which the partner is trying to manage. While such a partner may also be interested in seeing the results of the firm as a whole, this does not actually form part of the management responsibilities. At a lower level still, any partner within a particular department ought to receive information on personal performance but might also find it useful to receive comparative information about other partners in the same department against whom a comparison might be beneficial. It is unlikely, however, to be beneficial to disclose detailed information on individual partners in other departments because this will only encourage a partner to look at the results of other people rather than to focus on the results that the partner in question is delivering. The information that is provided to individual partners should probably also be provided to individual fee earners because it is only with financial information that individual fee earners can appreciate the financial effect of their day-to-day actions.

Historically the main reason for the lack of management information has been the difficulty in producing it on a timely basis. Prior to the rapid explosion of the use of information technology within firms the necessary management information was simply not available. Nowadays in many firms there is a new problem emerging being the huge volumes of management information that are produced from computer systems. It is probably right when considering management reporting to try to keep monthly management information sheets down to one sheet of A4 paper, or two sheets at the most, so that it is possible for all fee earners to concentrate on key measures and not to lose sight of those important areas. Many times in recent years partners have been given a thick print out at the start of the month containing useful financial information but such information has gone unnoticed because it is lost among the reams of paper which surround it.

Another important aspect of introducing a more specific management reporting system is the need to provide training to those partners and fee earners who will be receiving management information. It is one thing for fee earners to receive information but it is quite another thing for them to understand that information and to know how to use it effectively. Some firms have started to distribute information without providing proper training. This can cause some panic within the firm, both because fee earners feel under pressure to use the information but do not know how to use it and also because they feel that there must be a major problem that has led to this need to distribute information even if this is not the case. When the format of this monthly management information sheet is being considered, it may be appropriate to provide training very early on so that all fee earners have an opportunity to contribute to the final format of the monthly sheets that are to be distributed.

An essential ingredient of any monthly management reporting sheet is that both budget and actual information should be provided. If the fee earner is simply provided with actual information this is of little value since it cannot be assessed without an understanding of what was expected. Equally, if a fee earner simply receives a budget but then does not receive any actual information, there is precious little point in having the budget in the first place. When establishing the budgets for individual fee earners it is therefore crucially important that the budget must be personalised and relate to each and every individual. If individual budgets are simply created by taking an average figure from across the firm then this is unlikely to be of great assistance. Fee earners who can beat this average budget will not be motivated to perform any better and those fee earners who have little chance of achieving the budget will be demoralised and perhaps demotivated by their inability to attain the required target.

The key aim in providing management information is that management should act swiftly to improve performance. It is therefore vitally important that management information which is produced should be distributed promptly to fee earners. For monthly management information it is therefore probably right to aim to distribute information within ten days of the month end if it is to be of real use. Indeed if the information is delayed any longer than this then much of the information may become out of date and will rapidly have less value to individual fee earners. In the past some firms have been so concerned to ensure that the information is entirely accurate that this has often led to an unnecessary delay in the distribution of the information. It may be right on occasions to distribute information to fee earners promptly, even if it is not 100% accurate, the speed of distribution often being even more important than knowing whether or not the information is 100% accurate.

It has been indicated above that perhaps a monthly management sheet should be no more than one or two pages of A4 paper in length. There is certainly no correct format for such a report but to design such a report is often very difficult if one starts with a clean sheet of paper. Figure 22 may well be of assistance but it is important to remember that such a sheet must meet the specific needs of an individual firm or an individual department: the proforma that follows is not supposed to be a correct format.

Figure 22   Monthly information sheet

March 1996 (April 1996) Year End...*Note*
1

Litigation group partners	Fee earners in group				
B Jones	A Andrews	R Thomas			
F Smith	J Black	M Walker			
L Roberts	C Brown				

F Smith		Actual	Budget	2/3
1.	Cumulative bills for the financial year to date	£378,491	£385,000	4
2.	Total bills for March only	£60,085	£35,000	5
3.	Recovery for the financial year to date	97%	95%	6
4.	Recovery for March	102%	95%	7
5.	Chargeable hours for March only	136.20 hours	110 hours	8
6.	Cumulative daily chargeable average to date	6.12 hours	5.3 hours	9
7.	Cumulative daily chargeable average to date for:			10
	J Black	4.27 hours	5.3 hours	
	C Brown	5.83 hours	5.3 hours	
8.	Total unbilled time (see detailed work in progress)	£318,478	—	11
9.	Unpaid bills:			12
	a: Total (see detailed debtors)	£174,965}	—	
	b: 7 months and over	£52,626}	—	
10.	Work in progress days	276 days	250 days	13
11.	Debtor days	152 days	100 days	14

Figure 22 refers to a number of notes which should be interpreted as follows:

Note 1   This is an information sheet which relates just to the litigation group. There are three partners in the group being Jones, Smith and Roberts. There are also five fee earners in the group being Andrews, Black, Brown, Thomas and Walker. The information that is going to be disclosed to these people will be information that relates just to this group and not to other parts of the firm.

Note 2   This sheet is specifically for one of the three partners, Smith. This sheet should be distributed to Smith who should probably also receive similar sheets relating to Jones and Roberts because it is more important that the litigation group as a whole achieves its target rather than just worrying about whether or not any one individual partner achieves a target for the year. The five fee earners in the group should receive the sheets for the three partners because this will contain information that is relevant to them. Depending on exactly how the accounting system operates, it may be appropriate to produce a sheet for each partner and for each fee

	earner if fee earners bill directly on their own account rather than for one of the partners.
Note 3	There are two columns throughout the information sheet which give actual information and budget information. As noted earlier in the chapter it is important that the budget information relates specifically to the individual fee earner and that this budget is not just an average which is used across the firm.
Note 4	The greatest limiting factor on profitability is the level of fees per partner and therefore it is of crucial significance that partners get as close as possible to their annual targets. The information provided here provides a running total throughout the year.
Note 5	Bills issued in the current month are disclosed to provide some immediate feedback on performance in the most recent month.
Note 6	Recovery for the financial year to date shows the proportion of work in progress that has been turned into bills. In this particular case actual performance has been 2% higher than budget. At first sight this may not seem significant but given that this particular partner is going to issue fees of approximately £400,000 over a year, to achieve a recovery of 2% higher than budget would deliver increased profits of £8,000 over the year. In other words this higher level of recovery against budget has reduced the cumulative short fall in fees delivered for the year to date.
Note 7	Recovery for the current month shows performance considerably above average and as in Note 5 provides information in relation to the most recent month. The most recent information is often important because it might provide more information on the likely trend for the future than is obtained by simply looking at the cumulative performance for 11 months.
Note 8	The information provided here states how many chargeable hours were recorded by Smith in the month of March. Smith exceeded his budget by 26.2 hours and obviously this is a positive variance.
Note 9	Perhaps more important than just knowing results for one month is to know the overall performance for the year to date and this information is provided here in a slightly different format. Another way of measuring chargeable hours is to look at the daily chargeable average over the year to date. In this case a target of 5.3 hours per day was set but the partner has achieved actual performance of 0.82 hours per day more. This apparently small level of performance over budget is in fact extremely significant because over a year as a whole this would lead to additional chargeable hours of perhaps 150 to 200 hours.

Note 10   Smith also receives information on the cumulative daily charge-able hours average for Black and Brown because it is assumed here that Black and Brown are under the direct responsibility of Smith. The other fee earners in the group would presumably be under the direct control of the other two partners and hence their names would appear on the sheet for James and Roberts in March. On reviewing these figures it is apparent that Brown is averaging 0.53 of an hour a day in excess of budget which is good, but unfortunately Black is averaging 1.03 hours a day less than budget which is an adverse variance. It is important for Smith to see the figures for the assistants that he controls as well as for his own performance. Just because Smith exceeds his own personal target does not mean that the group as a whole will exceed its target and it is therefore important that Smith makes sure that Black has as much work as possible.

Note 11   The information here shows the gross unbilled work at the end of March for Smith. This figure can be compared with the bills issued for the year to date to give an immediate understanding of the speed with which bills are being issued. It may be appropriate to provide some further analysis of this unbilled time, for example to highlight any work in progress that is over 6 months old.

Note 12   The information provided here explains the uncollected bills at the end of March. Further analysis is also provided to show the amount of bills outstanding which are over 7 months old.

Note 13   While the information explained in Note 11 is meaningful in that it gives a monetary value to the unbilled time, perhaps a more useful measure for controlling work in progress is to calculate the amount of outstanding work in progress as a number of days. In this particular case the budget for Smith was to issue bills within 250 days of doing the work but in fact he is not issuing bills for an average of 276 days.

Note 14   The debtor days figure explains the number of days credit that clients are taking before settling bills. The target for this particular partner was 100 days but in fact clients are taking 152 days to settle bills.

The monthly information sheet in Figure 22 should probably be distributed to the three partners in the group and also to Black and Brown and perhaps also the other fee earners in the group. If the information on the sheet was discussed by Smith, Black and Brown at the start of April then it is likely that, between the three of them, some immediate positive action could be taken.

The review of this sheet would probably highlight the following:

(a)   Bills issued for the 11 months to date are almost on target and so there only needs to be a reasonable level of billing in the final month of the year.

(b)   The recovery percentage being achieved by this partner is certainly well above average and was particularly high in March. The three recipients of the information sheet could usefully review how best they can maintain this high recovery rate and to see whether there is any scope for increasing it still further.

(c)   Smith has achieved in March and over the year to date a high level of chargeable hours and this is considerably in excess of budget. The same can also be said for Brown but the opposite is true for Black. A useful discussion might now take place on how the workloads can be organised to ensure that Black is kept busier. In all groups there is always a danger that partners hang on to too much work for themselves and in so doing fail to delegate work to a more cost effective level.

(d)   The ability of Smith to issue bills and collect cash once bills have been issued is extremely poor. In total Smith was budgeting to allow clients 350 days total credit including debtor and work in progress days but is in fact operating at a level of 428 days credit. To allow clients over a year of credit is clearly unacceptable and the three fee earners should now make a conscious effort to accelerate the speed of issuing bills and put more pressure on clients to settle those bills once they have been issued.

If such information is not disclosed to partners and fee earners then there is little that a partner or fee earner can do during a month other than carry on providing the best possible legal service to the clients.

9

The Development of Personal and Management Skills

Introduction

This book has concentrated on the way in which any firm should set about increasing its profitability and has explained the mechanics of profitability and provided some bench-marks for performance. A book on profitability would not, however, be complete without some consideration of the management of people. A law firm is a service business and the service that is provided is dependent upon the quality of the people and the way in which they are managed.

As has been established in chapter 4, the most profitable firms will have a relatively large number of fee earners for each equity partner so that each equity partner is not just generating profit for himself but is also having profit created by other fee earners in his team. Such a strategy of increasing the size of pyramid beneath each partner would clearly be reckless if the partners concerned were unable to manage the pyramid effectively and to obtain the best from all people. It is, of course, possible to make a loss on every member of the pyramid if the people are badly managed or if there is insufficient work to keep these people busy.

Significance of partners' management skills

It is essential that partners develop and display strong management and personal skills. If such role models are in place then it is likely that other fee earners will display these skills quickly as they progress up through the ranks. It has to be said that historically there has not been a great deal of emphasis on these skills in many law firms and that at present these skills are unlikely to develop naturally. Partners who have been successful for a number of years will frequently be extremely sceptical about the value of training in these areas and yet it is often only after receiving the training that partners begin to appreciate that there is still scope for improvement.

Management of staff, whether they be fee earners or secretarial and support staff, is essential. Many solicitors back away from management because they believe it to be non-chargeable. This may be the case if one is talking about the management of the practice but if one is talking about the management of fee earners on individual matters then this time should be chargeable. Indeed, by delegating work to more junior members of staff and by controlling this work through sound management, it should be possible to provide a service to clients at a lower cost than would otherwise be necessary if the work was undertaken just by a partner. Management time under these circumstances is therefore chargeable. A partner sitting at the top of a very large pyramid is theoretically able to be fully chargeable even if the partner never undertakes any detailed work on a transaction.

It is highly unlikely that the necessary skills will develop within a firm without some training. The fee earners will generally be too busy to stop to consider the skills that need to be developed, let alone find the time to consider how best the skills can be developed. It should also be recognised that training is not always the answer and that it might just be the catalyst to any change that needs to take place. Nobody is going to become a good manager simply as a result of a course but the course may well provide useful ideas which can then be put into practice. It is extremely important therefore when considering training in this area to ensure that a mechanism has been established to follow the training through and to ensure that the principles discussed in the training are subsequently followed through in practice.

What specific skills are needed?

A question that is often asked within firms and by management consultants is, 'what are the skills required by successful partners?'. The following is a list of some of the most commonly given answers:

focus on clearly defined goals;
commercial approach and understanding of the business;
well organised;
strong technical skills;
ability to motivate staff;
good delegation;
provide clear instructions;
know how to supervise effectively;
provide objective and regular feedback;
understand the importance of teams;
know how to lead others.

It is worth spending a little time considering the above list to establish exactly what is required.

1 Focus on clearly defined goals

No manager will ever be able to manage a team effectively if no time has been given to focus on clearly defined objectives. As was considered earlier in this book, every firm should have a clear business plan which sets out objectives for the firm over a period of perhaps 3 to 5 years. From this plan, which should be agreed by the partners, individual partners should be able to identify the things that they need to achieve in order to achieve the overall business plan. Without such focus it is all too easy for any partner to fail to make big strides simply because there is always more than enough work to be done.

The individual goals for partners can normally be established through the creation of detailed job descriptions. It is important that these job descriptions are written documents because they can also then be used as a measure of appraising individual partner performance at the end of each year.

2 Commercial approach and understanding of the business

All too many lawyers simply aim to be the best lawyer. While a great deal of satisfaction can be derived from providing an outstanding legal service to clients, this alone will not necessarily make the firm profitable. It is extremely important therefore that all partners and fee earners have a strong understanding of how a law firm operates and hence appreciate the effect of their day-to-day actions on the profitability of the firm.

There is a growing trend in many firms to ensure that fee earners have a stronger commercial understanding of individual clients and the sector in which they operate. Without such knowledge it will be extremely hard for solicitors to identify the precise needs of clients and the solicitor may simply appear as somebody who is trying to offer legal services rather than being somebody who is trying to find solutions to client needs.

3   Well organised

Partners need to be able to manage their own work as well as the work of others and are likely to have a large number of outstanding items at any time. Outstanding matters will include both client work and non-client work and over a period of time it is important that all matters are dealt with effectively.

Poor time management can lead to excessive working hours, unnecessary stress, professional indemnity risk and high staff turnover. The combined effect of these problems is almost certain to reduce the profitability of any firm.

Fee earners must learn how to manage their time. The simplest thing that needs to be done is for all fee earners to produce a To Do list which details all outstanding matters. There is a clear difference between a To Do list and a wish list. A wish list is something that is produced by a fee earner on a periodic basis which sets out the tasks that the fee earner would like to undertake. Such lists are not normally comprehensive and once a fee earner has got stuck into a particular item on the list other items suddenly raise their heads and the fee earner immediately has to change direction and do something else, often something which is more urgent. A To Do list is supposed to be a comprehensive list of outstanding items which the fee earner can use to manage time. The benefit of a comprehensive To Do list is that fee earners can start to use their minds for doing things rather than for remembering what needs to be done. There is also the added benefit that at the end of the day a fee earner can go home and switch off knowing that there is nothing left that needs to be done on the To Do list.

If a To Do list is going to be kept up to date then it needs to be a working document. Ideally the To Do list should be carried round with a diary and whenever a new matter arises it should immediately be entered onto the To Do list if it cannot be dealt with immediately. For example, if a piece of correspondence in the morning's post could not be dealt with immediately it should be written down on the To Do list as a reminder that it is outstanding. Equally, when a client or someone from within the firm telephones and asks the fee earner to undertake a particular task then, if this cannot be dealt with immediately, it should go down on the list as a reminder of another outstanding item. Once a discipline has been established for capturing items on the To Do list, the To Do list can then be used to control time. Many fee earners start with good intentions when using a To Do list but often slip into bad habits when they get under greater pressure. This is a big mistake because it is at times of increased pressure that a To Do list would be most invaluable.

Once a To Do list has been created it is possible to prioritise work in a sensible manner. All too many fee earners do things that are quick and hence easily accomplished, fun to do, easy, or work for clients who shout the loudest. While at times this might lead to fee earners doing what they should be doing this would certainly not always be the case. When looking at a To Do list and deciding what should be done next there are two matters which need to be considered. The first matter is the urgency of the task. The second matter, which may conflict with the first consideration, is the importance of the task. Urgency and importance are not the same thing. Something can be both urgent and important but equally things can be either important or urgent. Urgent items are things which have a pressing deadline. Important items are those things which matter and which will have a significant influence. Importance is immediately understood when thinking about clients. Some clients are more important than others. It is necessary to understand that non-chargeable work can be just as important as fee earning work.

All fee earners need to develop technical skills, management skills and marketing skills. It is important that this is achieved if a firm is to be profitable. Failure to attend to such development and to concentrate too much in the short term on extra chargeable time will often be counterproductive in the medium term.

The maintenance of a To Do list should ensure that proper planning is undertaken and that sufficient time is devoted to important items as well as urgent items. Important items should not always be left until they become urgent because this will often mean that such tasks are not dealt with effectively.

4   Strong technical skills

Every lawyer needs to be at least competent at the work he undertakes. Without such competence it will be extremely difficult to operate profitably and there will always be the danger of exposure to negligence claims. Technical training should therefore be focused on the precise needs of individual lawyers. Training to meet these needs can be dealt with on in house courses or through the attendance of public courses.

Most learning happens on the job, and not through the attendance of courses or by reading books. Senior fee earners must accept that they have a responsibility to train other staff, and they should appreciate that this will lead to greater efficency.

Many firms put all their efforts into developing technical skills and do not pay sufficient attention to the other areas which require development.

5   Ability to motivate staff

All partners and fee earners with responsibility for junior staff must know how to motivate. If such people are good at delegating, supervising and appraising but have not yet learnt the art of motivation, then they will never extract the very best from their staff.

Motivation is a complex issue because what motivates someone today may not have motivated the person a year ago and will not necessarily motivate the person in the future. Two useful theories on motivation have been developed by Maslow and Herzberg.

Maslow believes that there is a hierarchy of needs. This means that people strive to climb to higher and higher levels and their motivation comes from the next level. Once a level has been reached then that level is no longer a motivating factor and will cease to be unless the individual falls back to below that level again. This situation can be understood when thinking about how lawyers develop in a firm.

Trainee solicitors are motivated by being made to feel a part of a team and by being trusted with important work. Trainees do not often look much beyond the training period, and their motivation is to obtain a position after qualification.

Newly qualified solicitors are usually less worried about acceptance and survival and are motivated by having new, interesting and challenging work.

Partners in firms may still obtain some motivation from doing new and challenging work but usually the motivating factors have changed. Partners are often motivated by the challenge of making teams work and of gaining recognition from staff, partners, clients and society as a whole.

Herzberg classified the things that motivate people into hygiene factors and motivating factors. Motivating factors are things which if applied properly result in greatly increased output by staff. They are high level actions. Herzberg believes that motivating factors will not work at all if the more basic hygiene factors are not already in place. An example will perhaps illustrate the point. A firm established a profit related bonus scheme for secretarial staff. This is established as a motivating factor and it is hoped that it will have a dramatic effect. The danger is that the motivating factor may have no effect if a hygiene factor, such as the fact that there are no coffee/tea facilities available in the office, has not been dealt with.

A lesson that can perhaps be picked up from these theories is that often solicitors over complicate motivation. They try to create very complex motivating factors without actually addressing the hygiene factors, and then they cannot understand why staff are not more highly motivated.

Money needs to be considered when understanding motivation. Money will motivate certain people at certain times but it is not a universal answer. Money is usually described as a hygiene factor. Underpaying people will result in sub standard performance, but over paying people will not necessarily improve their motivation. Money is an important motivator for six weeks each year; for the two weeks before the annual pay review and for the four weeks after.

Given that different people are motivated in different ways and that everybody changes, there are no quick remedies. Motivating people happens by actions and not by thoughts. Good motivators do something to motivate staff.

The following list provides a few practical suggestions as to what could be tried to motivate fee earners and secretaries.

Fee Earners	Secretaries
Ask them — they might help you!	Ask them — they might help you!
Interesting work	Be polite
New work	Keep diaries up to date
Take interest	Public praise
Proper appraisal	Advise of whereabouts
Supervision	Teach new skills
Client contact	Introduce to clients
Regular meetings	Take to some meetings
Recommend to others	Planning meeting at start of each day
Budgets and targets	Proper appraisals
Public praise	Provide clear instructions
Environment	Be available to support
Teach new skills	Budgets and targets
Provide training	Environment
etc. etc.	etc. etc.

Looking at these lists, it is obvious that most of the items could be described as hygiene factors rather than motivating factors.

6   Good delegation

Often in professional firms it is apparent, when all aspects of work are added together, that it is the partners who are the busiest and as one looks down the hierarchy there is a gradual decline in the volume of work and the pressure at each level. Ideally there should be even levels of work at all levels but this can only be achieved if partners and senior fee earners are willing to delegate more effectively.

It is interesting to stop and consider why delegation often does not take place as readily as one might have expected. The following list of barriers to delegation considers the issue both from the delegator's and the delegatee's perspective:

Barriers to the delegator	Barriers to the delegatee
Quality	Rubbish work
Loss of control	Poor instructions
Efficiency/cost	Lack of support
Deadlines	Interference
Client requirements	
Lack of resources	

On reviewing the above list it is perhaps apparent that very few of these reasons for lack of delegation actually hold water. Most of the reasons in these lists exist because of the process of delegation and do not represent real barriers if the process is carried out effectively. The only barriers which hold water are deadlines, a lack of resources and on some occasions client requests although this is often used as an excuse for not delegating.

The practical skill of delegating involves a number of steps, none of which are complicated but many busy practitioners often do forget one or more of these steps which means that work is delegated badly. The following points should be considered when delegating:

Not letting go versus abdication
People who are new to management often fail to let go sufficiently and are seen as interfering by the delegatee. Once the delegator realises that this is not working there is then often a tendency to overreact the other way and in effect to abdicate. Delegating a piece of work and then walking away from it will not work either and eventually most managers work out where delegation lies, being somewhere between abdication and not letting go. Any solicitor could usefully ask fee earners to describe their delegation style in terms of whether they fail to let go or abdicate.

Provide clear instructions
It is quite frightening to consider how much time is wasted each year in firms through poor instructions which can also lead to tensions being created between members of a team. Clear instructions are likely to mean that the job is done right first time leading to lower costs and higher profits. The most common mistake made by managers is that when giving instructions they provide an overview of what is required but little more in terms of detailed instruction. Too much knowledge is assumed in the person who is being assigned the task and the person, when trying to complete the task, consequently fails. A contributory factor to this state of affairs is that the person handing out the work does not

want to be seen to be talking down to the person who is being instructed and hence assumes a higher level of knowledge than actually exists.

The correct technique for providing clear instructions is to provide an overview and then go through the task in a number of stages in far more detail. For example, having given an overview it may then be appropriate to break the task down into perhaps five chunks. For each chunk the manager should talk through what is required but then before moving on to the next step should ask the other party to explain what needs to be done and to see if there are any questions. The person providing the instructions should not move onto the second chunk until he or she is happy that the other party totally understands what is required. There is clearly a big difference between understanding how to do a task and having the knowledge to do the task.

Precise requirements
It is all too easy for somebody who is delegating to fail to communicate the exact requirements of the task. Everyone has experienced a situation when they think they have performed a task but then they are told that they have completely missed the point. When delegating it is therefore important to ensure that the delegatee has a very clear understanding of the precise requirements which may actually mean providing an example of the sort of document that needs to be produced.

Clearly agreed budgets and deadlines
When delegating work it is essential to provide both a budget and deadlines, given that once the assignment is completed some feedback should be provided. It is important to know how much time is anticipated for the task. When providing feedback it is one thing to say that somebody has performed well or badly on a task, it is quite a separate issue to talk about the efficiency in achieving this result. Failure to give somebody a budget will often mean that they do not know when to come and ask for further help because they do not know whether they should yet have resolved issues for themselves or not. Deadlines are also important because people have to schedule more than one task at the same time.

Rather than just having one deadline at the end of the assignment it is usually correct when briefing to list out a number of deadlines at which times the progress of the work can be reviewed. By operating in this way the delegator remains in control of the work and is not reliant upon the delegatee coming back when there are problems.

Take an interest in the work being delegated
Often the work that is delegated is fairly routine in the eyes of the delegator and this may be seen by the delegatee as being unimportant work. It is therefore important that the delegator always takes time to explain the task properly and shows an interest throughout the task to maintain the motivation of the delegatee.

Provide immediate feedback
To undertake an assignment and to receive no feedback is always de-motivating. Feedback should consider both what was done well and what was done less well. Areas requiring improvement should always be tackled with practical suggestions as to how such improvement can be achieved.

Feedback is essential when delegating because the delegatee knew something about the task before attempting it but will learn from the delegator by seeing exactly what needs to be done to bring the task to completion. If no feedback of this sort is provided then the delegatee learns nothing and therefore makes no progress and becomes frustrated.

7 Knows how to supervise effectively

Many senior partners and fee earners believe that all they have to do to supervise staff effectively is to tell them that 'my door is always open'. Supervision, as with all other management skills, is a practical skill that involves spending time and is not simply a state of mind. The most common mistake made is that solicitors do not find time to supervise staff effectively.

Those who do remember to supervise staff fall into a common trap of asking a question that does not provide a useful reply. Probably the most common approaches used when supervising staff are, 'how are you doing?' or 'is everything okay?'. Both of these questions will probably get an answer of 'fine', irrespective of whether there is good or bad progress. When supervising staff it is therefore important to ask open questions which get people to talk about what they have been doing. It will quickly become apparent if there are any problems and at this stage it may be appropriate to look at the detailed documentation that has been produced. If, however, it is clear that good progress is being made then the partner can leave the fee earner to carry on.

Supervision is in effect an insurance policy. With no supervision or no insurance there is a great risk that work can be misdirected and time wasted. It is equally possible to be over insured, or for too much supervision to take place:

all of the time spent supervising may not achieve anything in itself if the person undertaking the task is able to complete the task unaided. A balance therefore needs to be achieved. The frequency of supervision needs to be determined and this ought to be in line with the amount of time that a fee earner is willing to risk being wasted.

If partners are going to become more effective at supervising staff then they must get into a routine and find time to supervise staff on a regular basis. There are perhaps two ways of dealing with this issue. The first is to agree, at the point at which work is first delegated, when work is to be supervised. Everybody will know at what stage work is to be reviewed and this should be quite effective. The alternative approach is to supervise people on a regular basis. This approach may be more relevant in a situation where a partner is supervising another fee earner who has a large number of files open at any time. The purpose of supervision is now not to deal with a specific matter but to review matters generally. If the second approach is to be adopted then it would probably make sense to supervise the fee earner at one of the natural breaks of the day, i.e., the start, the middle or the end of the day since it is highly unlikely that anyone could get into a routine of supervising someone in the middle of the morning or the middle of the afternoon which are the two main working chunks of the day.

8   Provide objective and regular feedback

In many firms fee earners, secretarial staff and support staff think that appraisal only happens once a year. It may well be that the formal appraisal only happens once a year but in any well managed firm appraisal should be an on-going process. If the process is managed properly then at the formal appraisal, which takes place once a year, there should be no shocks because there should already be good communication taking place between managers and subordinates.

An effective appraisal is one at which the appraisee receives objective feedback on past performance and understands precisely what is required in the future. In other words an appraisal should look backwards, and things can be learnt from looking backwards, but the emphasis of the appraisal should be directed towards the future and positive development.

For an appraisal to be effective there must be thorough preparation by both the appraiser and the appraisee because if either party does not prepare thoroughly then the appraisal discussion itself cannot be effective. Different firms use different forms to prepare people for appraisals. There needs to be a balance between providing some structure and at the same time not being over prescriptive. Appraisal forms used by different firms range from a blank sheet of paper that is certainly not over prescriptive to appraisal forms that are 10 pages long with a series of questions that will not be applicable to a great many people. The key to any paperwork that is prepared before any appraisal is that it should focus on the role that the person being appraised currently performs and how that role is to develop in the future. Such an assessment may best be done by identifying the main responsibilities and main activities of the individual under review.

The preparation for an appraisal is in itself of very limited value. The purpose of such preparation is to ensure that the face-to-face discussion is as productive as possible. Many lawyers are worried about the face-to-face discussion because they are fearful of conflict with other members of staff and therefore fail to discuss key issues which really should be raised.

If both parties in an appraisal agree on matters raised during the appraisal then there is unlikely to be any conflict. The reason why conflict arises during appraisals is because the perception of the two parties may differ. It is therefore important in any appraisal interview that the appraisee should be asked to talk at length first so that when the appraiser comes to provide some feedback it has already been established what the appraisee thinks. By following this sequence of events the appraiser is then able to provide feedback in an objective way but in the full knowledge of what the appraisee believes to be the case.

The final point for consideration in the appraisal process is to determine who talks most during each appraisal. In practice, it is often found that the appraiser is talking for two thirds of the time but the commonly held view is that ideally the appraisee should be talking for two thirds of the time. Where the appraiser is talking for the majority of the time such an appraisal is likely to be too one-sided and the appraisee may not ultimately agree with the conclusions of the appraisal.

9   Understand the importance of teams

Historically, many firms of solicitors could be described as a group of sole practitioners who chose to share the overheads. Recently an increasing number of firms have become more and more sophisticated in trying to develop teams within the firm. The potential for a team is that it could produce more than the sum of the parts but there is a danger in any team that it actually delivers less than the sum of the parts. Working in teams will therefore not provide an automatic benefit to the firm, such benefit will only stem from effective teams. Some other key benefits that arise from working in successful teams are as follows:

greater commitment;
faster learning;
greater flexibility;
greater efficiency;
improved morale;
better use of specialists etc.

A great deal of research has been undertaken on the development of successful teams and it is important to distinguish between the role of the leader and the other team players. The role of the leader will be dealt with under the next heading.

A successful team will have a combination of strengths spread across the team players such that in total the team has all of the required strengths. The fact that individual members of the team may be weak in certain areas is an irrelevance provided that the other members of the team possess and use the required strength. This approach to teams might seem fairly obvious but all too often one finds in law firms appraisal systems which concentrate on correcting weaknesses rather than playing to strengths.

Although it is becoming less significant, many law firms remain very hierarchical in their structure. When considering the roles that different members of the team should adopt, hierarchy should not be a factor. For example, each team will need somebody who can coordinate the affairs of the team and who is able to chair meetings. In many firms the person who adopts this role should be the most senior person within the group but this clearly is not necessary. The most junior member of the team may well have the skill to chair meetings and if this is the case than this is the right person to carry out the task. Another example where hierarchy can cause problems in teams is that every team needs somebody who is going to try to think of new approaches to matters which are to be tackled. In many professional firms more junior people would think twice about raising suggestions for fear that they may be ridiculed. If, however, such a junior person is good at coming out with new and creative ideas then the junior should not be inhibited by more senior people who lack such skills.

Different people have different aptitudes for the various roles required in team working. It is important for everybody to identify the best way in which they can contribute to teams and then to try to work with other people who have the necessary complementary skills. People who have the same skills and who work together in a team will often clash. For example, somebody who has a great sense of urgency and who often thumps the table and becomes irritated because progress is not being made, will often fall out with somebody else with the same personality type. This is because people understand the role that they enjoy performing and they do not like other people to try to carry out the role for them.

A number of well researched psychometric tests have been developed which can establish the contribution that individual people can make in a team context. While there is a danger that firms may place too much reliance on the output of such tests, it is dangerous for any firm to ignore this aspect of working if highly successful and profitable teams are to be created.

10   Know how to lead others

The final aspect of management that needs to be addressed is the role of the leader in any team. The role of the leader is to make the team work as effectively as possible. The leader may or may not be the most senior member of the group but in most professional firms this is normally the case.

So what styles of leadership exists? In very simple terms leaders can direct people or alternatively they can be indirect in their leadership. A direct style of leadership at the most extreme case involves telling people what to do, whilst a slightly less direct method of leadership would be to provide guidance to somebody else. When a leadership style becomes non-directive then a gentle form of this style would be to offer guidance while a pure non-directive style would involve helping somebody to solve their own problems.

It is maybe worth considering how fee earners would prefer to be managed. Would they prefer to be told what to do in a directive style, or would they prefer to be helped to work things out for themselves in a non-directive style? Maybe the first thing that should be realised is that different people will respond well in different situations and there is no correct style of leadership. Intelligent people will normally say that they would prefer to be helped to solve their own problems rather than always being told what to do. If one reviews the style of leadership that exists in most professional firms, however, the majority of people still lead more by telling people what to do than by helping others to solve their own problems. There would appear therefore to be a need for a shift of some size towards non-directive styles of leadership.

Many people believe that whether a directive or non-directive style should be used is determined by the relative seniority of the two parties who are working together. This is not the case and the correct style should be determined by the relative level of the two parties involved and also the nature of the work being undertaken. Consider the way in which a partner leads a secretary. The partner has just returned from a client meeting to the office and instructs the secretary to type some notes of the meeting, to obtain some information from a third party and to arrange a further meeting. The secretary will probably be quite happy with this direct style of leadership. If, however, the partner wants to advise the secretary about a poor aspect of her performance, then the same style of leadership may not be productive. Simply to tell the secretary about the poor aspect of performance may result in the secretary immediately putting up a defence to the issue. A better approach may be to be non-directive and to ask the secretary to discuss the aspects of her performance that are good and the aspects of her performance that are less good. Provided the secretary can recognise for herself the problem that needs to be addressed then there is more likely to be some constructive movement.

Another interesting example of leadership styles revolves around the way in which free earners deal with clients. When a client comes for advice from an experienced partner there is a danger that the partner has heard about the situation before and immediately tells the client what to do. While this may be effective it may equally be more effective in some cases to encourage the client to rationalise the problem fully for himself because in this way there may be greater commitment to action. If one then considers the position of a trainee going into a meeting with a client to provide some advice, it is pretty unusual to find a trainee telling a client what to do and it is far more likely that the trainee, despite having looked up an answer, will start by asking the client what the client thinks should happen. This may work with a client but equally the client may be infuriated by such an approach because all the client wanted was to be told what to do.

There is nothing particularly profound in any of the above and all the items listed are really common sense. Honesty is important when assessing people's personal and management skills. People are unlikely to change their behaviour until it can be demonstrated with examples that there are areas where improvements could be made.

10

The Role of Client Care in Profitability

Throughout this book it has been stressed that the biggest constraint on profitability is the size of the fee portfolio for each partner. The development of fee portfolios for each and every partner is therefore of crucial importance in every firm.

1 Reviewing reality

Far too many practitioners kid themselves as to why they are not more successful in gaining work. Before one embarks on any new campaign it is important to be honest with oneself and to review past experiences and the present position. While it is possible to be unlucky on an individual pitch for new work there is no such thing as permanent bad luck.

It is worth stopping to consider exactly where clients come from. For many fee earners this is not something that is considered on a regular basis as there always appears to be more client work to be done. Figure 23 provides a simple overview of how clients are generated.

Figure 23   Where do clients come from?

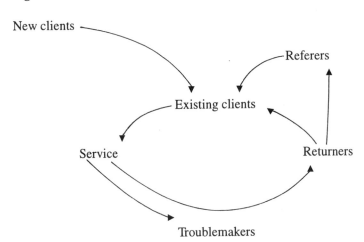

In many firms too much effort is directed towards trying to attract brand new work to the practice. When an enquiry comes in from an unknown party it is often far too tempting to drop everything and put in an extra special effort in the hope of winning this new piece of work. It is extremely difficult to establish whether this is a genuine request for a quote or simply a matter of obtaining an alternative fee quote in order to put pressure on existing providers. As a result the time could be completely wasted.

When one considers existing clients, however, they could either build or damage a practice. The key factor affecting the outcome is the level of service which is provided. A dissatisfied client may well become a troublemaker. A troublemaker is extremely damaging to a firm because when someone is dissatisfied they not only remove their business but they also start to tell other people about their dissatisfaction. Bad publicity caused in this way is clearly very damaging in the medium to long term for a firm.

A client who is happy with the service will become a returner, remaining a client for the following year or for the next transaction. It is worth noting, however, that just because a client returns and allows a firm to carry on acting it may not in fact be fully satisfied with the service that is being provided.

A key aim for any firm is to try and turn a returning client into a referrer of new work. Whenever a partner reviews his list of clients it is probable that only a very small minority of clients actually refer new business. One conclusion that could be drawn is that only a few clients are genuinely satisfied and are willing to recommend the firm to other people. Of course, another conclusion could be that there are many more clients who would be willing to refer a firm to new clients but they do not do so because they have not been asked or they perceive that the firm is already to busy.

Before embarking on any new marketing campaign it is important to analyse the level of service that is being provided to the existing client base or that will be provided to future clients. If one is going to turn clients into referrers of new work then it is necessary to 'superplease' them. To superplease clients firms must do more than simply please them, firms must exceed clients' expectations. Figure 24 illustrates how a client's expectations are exceeded. Client expectations are always growing because when one firm starts to offer a new service, thereby superpleasing a client, other firms quickly mirror this level of service, it becomes the expected standard, and no longer serves to superplease the client. Firms then have to develop new ways of superpleasing clients.

Figure 24   Superpleasing clients

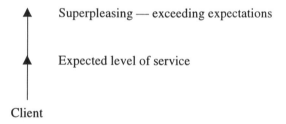

Superpleasing — exceeding expectations

Expected level of service

Client

So how is it possible to superplease clients? The following is a list of some of the ideas that are often suggested:

sending christmas cards;
providing a technically sound service;
taking clients out to lunch;
organising seminars;
sending news letters;
providing tax cards;
seeing clients on a regular basis.

Every client is different but it is doubtful that any of the above will do more than simply satisfy an existing client. It is perhaps unlikely that any of these activities will superplease clients. What is needed is something that is original or different; something that will distinguish one firm from the opposition. Firms are becoming increasingly innovative but some of the following might be possibilities or triggers to other ideas;

sending birthday cards;
sending postcards from holiday;
calling in on clients for an update;
sending clients copies of newspaper/magazine articles which will be of interest;
phoning clients every month, even if they don't contact you, to try to be proactive;
knowing the secretaries of your clients as well as the client.

Honesty — client surveys

It has now been established that it is always important to understand how clients perceive the service provided by the firm. It is all to easy to be fooled into believing that a better service is being provided than is actually the case. Equally, it is very easy to be negative and to think that the level of service being provided is inferior to that provided by competitors and that clients are therefore dissatisfied. The best way of determining a true level of satisfaction is to organise a client survey. Figure 25 sets out a simple client satisfaction questionnaire that could form the basis of such a survey.

Figure 25   Client satisfaction questionnaire

Name ....

1.   How do you rate the following aspects of our service to you?

	Excellent	Good	Acceptable	Poor	Very poor
a) Speed	☐	☐	☐	☐	☐
b) Quality	☐	☐	☐	☐	☐
c) Value for money	☐	☐	☐	☐	☐

	Yes	No
2. Are our staff courteous and polite at all times?	☐	☐
3. Do we answer the telephone promptly?	☐	☐
4. Are you sufficiently satisfied with our services to recommend us to others?	☐	☐

5.   Which aspects of our service do you especially like?

....

....

6.   Which aspects of our service do you dislike?

....

....

7.   If there was one extra thing we could do for you (however small) what would it be?

....

....

8.   Do you have any other comments to make about our service?

....

....

Perhaps the most important question on the survey, or when talking to clients generally is 'if there is one thing that we could do to improve the service, however small, what would it be?'. If one refuses to accept the answer 'nothing', but insists that the client says something, then one will learn something about the service and the way in which it can be improved. If the recommendation is implemented, clients will become far more satisfied with the service because they will appreciate that the firm is making every effort to serve them properly. Only when clients appreciate that the firm is making this extra effort will they be likely to refer the firm automatically to new clients or to make such referrals if asked.

Do clients 'buy' or do you 'sell'?

Before developing a marketing strategy it is important to review the culture of the firm with regard to marketing and selling. There is a huge difference between trying to sell products and services to clients and helping clients to buy the services that they require. Many partners and staff in professional firms simply go out to clients with a list of products and services that are available and try to match these products and services to clients needs. Not surprisingly, when this approach is taken, it is fairly easy to antagonise clients by offering them services which they do not believe are appropriate or necessary. The correct approach must be to listen to clients, to understand their needs, and only then to make suggestions as to how the firm can help.

Such a shift in emphasis may take a while to achieve, but ultimately partners and staff will find marketing and selling easier because there will be less selling involved than with the existing system.

2   Internal communications

Initial plans and involvement of everybody

Marketing and selling are more likely to be successful if they are undertaken on a team basis rather than by a group of individuals who are all trying to achieve success on their own. The creation of a team is likely to generate the intangible asset of team spirit. Many practitioners when receiving their first defeat on a new marketing campaign may be inclined to give up and to move on to another opportunity. However, a setback faced by a team is likely to be reviewed sensibly and further attempts will be undertaken. Equally, when a team is successful it is often more rewarding to share that success with other people than to achieve success just on your own.

The creation of a team before marketing is undertaken is important. By ensuring that as much information as possible is gathered and by involving more people, greater input, knowledge and competence are likely to be generated.

It is often quite surprising how much knowledge and experience exists within a firm and individuals within a firm may recognise only a small part of that knowledge and experience.

Service versus industry specialisation

When considering marketing strategies and methods it is important to focus on what is being offered. Is it proposed to offer a particular service across a wide range of industries or is a firm aiming to offer a range of services to a specific industry? The final strategy, which is perhaps inappropriate because it is too narrow, is to offer a specific service to a specific industry. Because this is so very specialist it is clearly going to reduce the chances of finding a large market.

Feedback sheets

Communication is important throughout a marketing campaign, not just when establishing a campaign initially. Communication on a regular basis will help to maintain momentum for the campaign among the individuals that are involved. Obviously, there are a number of ways in which feedback can be provided to members of the team. A popular method is for the creation of a regular feedback sheet. A member of the team is appointed as the person responsible for the preparation of the sheet and everybody involved in the project is requested to forward pieces of information not to person for consolidation into a monthly or quarterly newssheet. The newssheet does not need to be glossy but simply has to provide information to participants of the team. The information should be presented in a positive light to maintain motivation throughout the exercise.

Another approach to providing feedback is to arrange regular meetings. The meetings do not need to last long but there is always a better understanding of issues if people hear other people talking about them rather than simply reading about the issues in newssheets, etc. The argument against meetings is that they represent non-chargeable time and when several people are involved there is a high cost. It is always worth bearing in mind, however, that not communicating effectively during a marketing campaign may result in the complete failure of that campaign and hence no benefit will arise from the marketing activity.

Depending upon the size and structure of the practice, it may be possible to use the IT system to help with the communication process, especially if everyone is networked.

Finally, communication should not just be about internally generated information. People in the team should be asked to review appropriate journals, newspapers and other professional publications to look out for relevant information which should be included in the feedback mechanisms.

3 Attending seminars

Check out the opposition

It is extremely difficult when entering a new market or when trying to develop a product to establish whether or not one has considered all of the potential problems and questions that clients may raise. An easy way of testing out a product or service is to attend conferences and seminars organised by others and to compare knowledge with that of others. Indeed, part of the initial research may be more easily undertaken by simply attending one or more courses rather than by spending far more time researching an area for oneself.

It is easy to forget that people who present courses to the public will always be concerned about the questions that are raised by delegates so that they will normally have done a vast amount of research before standing up to speak.

Attend industry conferences

Research into a particular sector or a particular product may be enhanced by attending conferences frequented by business people rather than solicitors. If a firm is considering marketing into a particular industry sector than it may be beneficial to attend conferences with people who work in that sector. While attending seminars with other lawyers may improve technical knowledge, it is not going to provide any direct marketing opportunities which could arise from meeting people from within a particular industry. Attending conferences with people from a particular industry will also help to provide an insight into the perceived problems that face the industry. Attending this sort of course or conference therefore provides the opportunity both to improve technical knowledge and also make some potentially useful contracts.

4 Training partners and staff

Culture

Marketing and selling are not issues that are discussed on a regular basis in professional firms, particularly below partner level. It is therefore important to identify who is expected to do the marketing and who is expected to do the selling. Marketing may be defined as the identification of target areas and the development of leads, while selling is the process of converting a lead into new work. Some firms are extremely good at marketing but do not fare so well at selling, while a few firms are good at the selling but not so good at marketing. To generate a constant supply of new work, care needs to be taken over both these aspects of the generation of new work.

Creating new work should not necessarily be left just to the partners. In particular, assistant solicitors may derive a great deal of benefit and enjoyment by becoming involved in the marketing aspects even if they do not have the confidence to go out and sell services directly to potential or existing clients. There is often a problem within a firm that assistant solicitors are worried about marketing and selling to existing clients because they feel that they may be treading on the toes of partners. For this problem to be overcome it is important for partners to discuss these issues with fee earners and to establish respective responsibilities. Fee earners in most firms see the generation of new work as being a partner responsibility and often partners reinforce this perception. In reality, most firms would like fee earners to become involved in this activity and it is probably worthwhile committing this to writing through detailed job descriptions. This will ensure that staff understand that partners do want staff to become involved in the process.

Client care training — changing procedures

Any firm, whatever its previous experience, can always improve the care that it provides to its clients. Improving client care is not a state of mind, it involves actions. Client care needs to be applied consistently by every member of the firm and not just by certain people, otherwise clients will perceive inconsistencies in the service. When developing a client care policy or updating an existing policy therefore, it is important that everybody in the office is involved. Simply imposing a new policy and telling everybody to comply with it may not lead to the desired result because people need to be committed to the changes if they are going to put them into effect.

One method of developing a client care policy may be to hold office meetings at which the principles of client care are explained and at which everyone is invited to contribute to a list of possible actions. It is normally quite remarkable how many bright ideas will come from different members of staff if they are encouraged to think laterally and positively about ways in which client service can be improved. Areas for discussion at such a meeting may include the following:

the way in which clients are greeted in reception by the receptionist and staff alike;
the speed with which clients get a response to correspondence;
the turnaround time for faxes, telephone answering and call back procedures;
the style of letters and reports that are issued to clients.

A mistake that is made by many firms is to tell clients about the changes they have introduced before they are really working within the office. For example, if a firm told its clients that they would always be welcomed with a smile when they arrived in reception and this did not happen, then this would be worse than not having told clients of this change at all. It is a mistake to try and do too much in one go, and greater long term benefit may be obtained by simply implementing two or three ideas per month and sticking with those ideas until they become routine. New ideas can then follow, and as new ideas are introduced those which have been put in place can be revealed to clients. This approach to client care can provide much satisfaction within the office but is also likely to be sustainable given that everybody in the office is invited to take part.

Budgets and targets

Training people to become better at marketing and selling would cost a firm both in terms of the time that is needed to be invested and in terms of cash costs. The cost does not need to be too high since much of the training can be provided internally. While it is probably a good idea for firms to try to do the training internally, it may help to bring in an outsider initially if for no other reason than to show the commitment of the partners and to generate some initial enthusiasm and momentum. Training in itself does not guarantee success and so it is important to develop measures to assess the benefit of the training that is provided. Firms can devise their own measures to assess the effectiveness of marketing and selling and the increased activity. Some of the following measures may be relevant to any firm:

the number of meetings attended;
the number of clients called proactively per month;
the number of articles written;
the amount of time spent at clients' premises;
the number of opportunities to quote;
the proportion of pitches that lead to new work;
new fees generated;
hours spent on marketing and selling.

Presentation skills

It is interesting to consider what it must be like to be a fly on the wall at a typical beauty parade for new work. Several firms are invited to pitch for the work and each thinks it has done a perfect job in preparing and delivering a presentation. A firm is presenting for work even if it is a one-to-one situation and simply involves sitting across a desk. Presentations also include standing up in front of a team of people from the target client. The biggest mistake made by most practitioners is that they have not rehearsed their presentation thoroughly beforehand. It is a great shame if the live presentation is no more than a dress rehearsal. A live presentation should be the best performance and should therefore always be made after the presentation has been rehearsed. Rehearsing presentations is not particularly time consuming or costly and will involve simply one or more people from within the office watching the presentation and making sensible observations.

Have the partners and fee earners in a firm been trained to present professionally? If they have not, then other firms will have a clear advantage even if the technical ability or substance of the service that is being sold is deficient. Some of the key skills of presentation that can be acquired through training are as follows:

effective movement;
full use of the voice;
getting started and maintaining interest;
controlling nerves;
eye contact and looking at the audience;
dealing with errs, ums and pauses;
designing and using visual aids;
dealing with difficult questions;
gaining participation and making it a two-way process.

Even if a solicitor has been trained to make presentations and there has been a rehearsal this does not guarantee success. One of the major reasons for not winning work is that when making the presentation the solicitor, through anxiety, makes no real show of commitment and enthusiasm for doing the work. It is important to have an extremely positive mental attitude when pitching for work. Body language is all important: smiling, looking confident, standing upright and talking confidently all add to the image being presented. Before going into the presentation it is important that adrenalin is running around the body. It is worth considering rolling up a newspaper and smashing it on a desk or wall a few times, shouting out 'we are going to win, win, win' as a way of getting into a positive frame of mind.

Beauty parades

When pitching for new work it will not always be necessary to stand up and make a formal presentation but increasingly this will be the case. The training skills mentioned above are important but there is also an element of psychology that needs to be considered. It is common sense that, when asked to pitch for work, you do as much research as possible beforehand and speak to as many people as possible at the target client before the presentation. The purpose of such research is to gain as full an understanding as possible of the client and of the services required. It is always possible, however, that one misunderstands the business or its needs or that one has actually been given incorrect information.

The approach to a presentation that is taken by most firms is to start by summarising the major needs that have been identified by the research and then to talk at some length as to how these needs can be satisfied. If a firm has identified needs that do not really exist, or has missed out on other important needs, then it will not be meeting the client's extact requirements. It is extremely important at the start of any presentation, therefore, to list the needs that have been identified and to ask the client for their observations before proceeding. If the prospective client explains that some of the perceived needs which have been identified are not actually relevant, then it is important to change the script and not to talk about those items any more. Equally, if the client identifies additional potential problems then these should be added to the list of things which are to be discussed. The prospective client will appreciate that if it is not part of a prepared presentation it will not be presented as professionally but will nevertheless be impressed by the fact that the firm is trying to service the needs of the client and is not simply trying to tell the client how clever or comprehensive is the range of services being provided by the firm.

The most important thing about beauty parades is coming first and not always coming second!

5 Pricing

Do not undervalue

An obvious way of generating work in a new area, or of increasing work in a particular sector, is by offering an extremely competitive price. While this may attract the attention of a potential client because a service is being offered that is cheaper than that being offered by competitors, it does not necessarily follow that in subsequent years, having obtained the work, it will be possible to force up the fees. The aim when generating new work is to generate profitable work and even if this does not happen in the short term it should flow through in the medium term. The whole effort will be wasted if each day, and indeed the years ahead, are filled with work that does not make an adequate level of profit.

Although it is a strategy, it is probably not an ideal one to pitch for new work on the basis of price. There are plenty of other strategies that can be adopted and if the right one can be found at a commercially sound price then this is likely to be more effective.

Pilot schemes

One often reads about firms who have 'low balled' to obtain new work. Low balling is designed to generate new work when it is believed that there will be no other way of gaining the work.

Some of the most common reasons given for not being awarded work are that either the price is too high or there was insufficient experience of the particular type of work. A method for overcoming both these objections is to reduce the price to make the tender extremely attractive and then, when you have won the first piece of work, you are able to quash the other objection, namely lack of experience, because you will then have a client in that particular sector.

An alternative strategy, which may be more successful, is to offer clients or potential clients a free service which is designed to test out the service that is being provided. The benefits of such an approach are numerous, including an opportunity to obtain some genuine feedback from a client, the opportunity to ask a client what they think the service is worth once they have seen it and the opportunity to refine the service before it is offered on a commercial basis. It may also be that, after working with a particular client and providing the client with a benefit, the client may be able to offer some useful leads to other potential clients. The final benefit of such an approach is that it is then possible to say that the service has been provided already to another client which immediately overcomes one of the primary objections described in the previous paragraph.

Build value

Many solicitors avoid the issue of pricing when quoting for new work. It is cleary a most important issue in the eyes of a potential client, and if the solicitor does not raise the issue first then the client will, and by doing so will take control of the conversation. The answer, therefore, is to strike first and raise the issue early in the discussions. By doing so it is possible to get a feel for the client's perceived value of the service before actually quoting formally. It is not too difficult to catch a client by surprise if early on in the discussions the client is asked if they would mind discussing fees. The obvious response is that they do not mind, and by giving such a response they put you in a position to take command of the discussion.

The most important thing to remember when quoting fees is to build value first. If one simply suggests a price then, whatever it is, it will seem expensive. The first thing that should be done, before any attempt is made to quote, is to describe exactly what is involved and the value that will accrue to the client from the services being provided. It may then actually seem more reasonable. For example, if a decorator is invited to come to your home and quote on the redecoration of the sitting room, one would probably think the fee was too great if he immediately quoted a figure of £750 plus VAT. However, if the decorator explained that he and his workforce would move all the furniture, protect the carpets, repair the squeaky floorboard, prepare the walls prior to applying the paint or hanging the wallpaper and apply the appropriate number of coats of paint to give a good finish, then when a final fee of £750 plus VAT is quoted the price might genuinely appear reasonable. With this approach it is more likely that the fee can be agreed rapidly.

It is important to go through this process with confidence. It is important to rehearse in advance of a meeting the value that is being provided to a particular client. If the same service or product is going to be provided to a number of different clients then it should not be too difficult to think through this process in advance. Having developed a clear understanding it is then simply a matter of repeating the benefits to a range of clients.

6   Marketing methods

Every firm must experiement with a variety of marketing methods: different methods will be right for different firms and for different practitioners. The following paragraphs summarise some of the main methods and techniques that should be considered.

Mailshots

It would be interesting to know quite how many mailshots the average business receives each year. This is probably the most popular method of marketing. Just because it is the most popular method of marketing, however, does not mean that it is always the most effective.

If a mailshot is to be effective it must be clearly targeted to named individuals and be very specific with regard to the services that are being offered. Mailshots must be followed up with a telemarketing activity as it is highly unlikely that a mailshot in itself will generate business. The purpose of a mailshot is normally to establish face-to-face contact with a named individual.

Many firms are becoming more and more creative with their mailshots in order to attract the attention of potential clients. A particular method that has attracted considerable interest is stage marketing. This involves sending a series of letters to a particular target client over a period of time. It works on the basis that an individual mailshot is unlikely to evoke a response but a succession of intriguing mailshots will raise interest and may ultimately lead to a response from the target organisation. An element of intrigue in such a process is clearly important but the goal at the end of the series of mailshots is simply to obtain a meeting.

The benefit of mailshots is that they are relatively inexpensive but of course they are a complete waste of money if no client contact or new work is generated.

The benefit of mailshots is that they are relatively inexpensive but of course they are a complete waste of money if no client contact or new work is generated.

Brochures

Most firms still require the need for one or more brochures to explain the services that they provide to clients. Brochures do not need to be glossy documents and can be a simple word processed document. The purpose of the brochure is to explain the service to a potential client in easy and understandable terms. In itself a brochure will probably not lead to new work. When trying to develop work in a particular niche area the creation of a brochure may suggest to clients a genuine commitment to the area rather than simply a firm sending out a speculative mailshot. Writing a brochure does also have the benefit of forcing the firm to think clearly about the service which it is offering.

If the production of brochures is selected as a marketing method it is important to ensure that they do not become out of date too quickly. The fewer dates that are mentioned the better, otherwise an economic print run may become obsolete in no time at all.

Advertising

A series of adverts is normally more expensive than a mailshot campaign and may lead to an even lower response rate. Any advert clearly needs to be eye catching as well as interesting if people are to take time to read it.

Careful preparation is essential to ensure that the size and nature of the readership is understood before placing any advertising material in a journal or magazine. It is also worth looking at a number of issues to establish whether or not the same companies advertise on a regular basis. Generally speaking, people will not advertise on a regular basis if there is no return generated. By looking at those people who advertise on a regular basis it is possible to gain a greater understanding of the type of advert that works and the kinds of services that the readership finds of interest.

An alternative approach is to talk to editors of magazines and trade journals about the possibility of providing advertorials, i.e., an article which is credited to the firm but which provides education to the reader. This may be cheaper than placing an advert and in many cases may be more effective as one will actually raise greater awareness of the issues amongst the readership than is possible in a small advertisement.

Presentation documents

Given the length to which firms go to obtain even the possibility of quoting, it is important that having obtained such an opportunity it is not wasted. Most pitches for work will involve a written letter or presentation document and may also involve a stand up presentation. The written documents that are submitted are often the only thing used to decide who gets the work, therefore the quality of both the content and the presentation of the document are of paramount importance. When entering a new sector or trying to generate new work it is, therefore, important that before starting the marketing one has considered the way in which proposals will be presented to prospective clients. To consider what these documents will look like only when you have been invited to tender may mean that there is insufficient time to prepare documents of sufficient quality.

There are numerous examples of solicitors marketing in particular sectors where they had the professional competence to undertake the work, but failed to get the work because the people against whom they were competing produced documents of a higher quality, in terms of content and presentation, even though they did not have the same level of skill available to provide the service within the firm.

Intermediaries

Earlier in this chapter the importance of clients becoming referrers of work was discussed. Another approach to marketing is to use third party referrers as intermediaries. If an intermediary such as a broker, banker or accountant, who deals with a large numer of clients in the sector that you are targeting, believes that the firm provides a better service than its competitors, then such intermediaries may well be minded to promote the services of the firm. It will be important to convince the intermediaries that the service is both different and better than that of others before such intermediaries would ever consider recommending your service. Many practitioners spend a great deal of time with intermediaries believing that they have convinced these intermediaries of the quality of their service but have become disenchanted with an intermediary who fails to generate any new work. The reason for lack of work flow may often be because the intermediary believes there are other people who provide a better service. Hence we go right back to where we started and the importance of looking to see whether or not the service that is being provided really would superplease clients.

Enjoy yourself

People normally only buy products and services from people whom they believe are successful in their own right. Successful people have an air of confidence about them which appears through written documents, body language and the way in which they communicate. It is unlikely that a solicitor can display this air of confidence if he or she does not enjoy marketing and the associated selling.

The style in which a solicitor markets must look natural and they must enjoy what they are doing or else success will only be limited. It is important to build up a bond with each and every client. This bond does not necessarily have to be work related but it is important to find a common interest. While this common interest may have no relevance whatsoever to the marketing, it often provides a way of building a bond between the target client and the solicitor who is trying to promote a particular service. When work is being obtained in a competitive situation, it is important to differentiate oneself from competitors and perhaps a way in which the marketing is undertaken is the most effective way of differentiating. Differentiation of the product or the service itself may be more difficult.

Whichever of the methods described above are used it is important for any firm to stick with a particular marketing campaign for a period of time. All too often one hears of the practitioner who chased after a new client in a new sector, but failed to get the work and immediately gave up on both the product and the sector, choosing to follow another lead with another product in another sector. To gain large amounts of work in a particular sector and to achieve a higher hit rate in attaining such work it is essential to stick to a particular product or sector for a period of time; perhaps a minimum of two years is really required. There may well be a number of knocks in the first 6 months. Work may only start to trickle in during the next 6 months and it is only in the second year of pushing a particular sector that work starts to appear in such large volumes that perhaps a new problem appears, namely having the resources available to deal with the work.

11

Tax Planning — Keeping the Profits

While a tax practitioner may want to read an entire book on tax planning, the emphasis of this book has been on the creation of a large profit and there is but one chapter on tax planning. Tax planning is not as much of an issue if there is no large profit in the first place. This chapter sets out to provide an overview of the main areas of tax planning for solicitors and is not supposed to be a tax manual. Planning areas highlighted are not supposed to be a comprehensive list and equally the areas described are not outlined in great detail but are simply there as ideas to be followed through in more detail as appropriate.

At times there may be a conflict between the aspirations of the partnership and of the individual partners. While it would be ideal if the partnership and the partners were always in accord, this will not always be the case and there are therefore often some difficult decisions to make.

Tax legislation changes on a regular basis and it is extremely rare for legislation to be retrospective. It is therefore important that planning is kept up to date so that opportunities are not missed, although one can never say with certainty that a better opportunity will not appear around the next corner.

The following are some of the most important areas for solicitors to consider together with some examples of how the planning can produce a tax saving.

Work in progress valuation

If work in progress is accounted for within the accounts then it represents additional income in the profit and loss account and a current asset in the balance sheet. Accounting for work in progress therefore increases accounting profits and taxable profits.

The most common method in solicitors' accounts is to account for work in progress on an earnings basis whereby work in progress is included in the accounts as it arises. However, such a basis accelerates the time at which profit is taken and therefore the paying of tax on that profit even though the profit may not yet have been realised as cash. This is the method that is especially preferred by the Inland Revenue as it complies with Generally Accepted Accounting Principles (GAAP).

An alternative basis adopted by a number of firms is a cash basis of accounting whereby the accounts are prepared on a cash basis and there is then no accounting for work in progress and debtors. When this basis is used there is a deferral before profit is recognised and tax is paid which leads to a cashflow advantage. The use of a pure cash basis is frowned upon by the Revenue and its use is seldom accepted for solicitors. Many barristers still adopt a pure cash basis because they are unable to sue for their fees. The alternative adopted by many solicitors is the conventional basis. Here, income is recognised when the appropriate fee account is rendered so whilst no work in progress is recognised, debtors are. A potential danger for a firm working on either the cash or conventional basis is that while there is a deferral of the tax liability it is important to retain sufficient cash in a partnershp to meet the potential liabilities or else the firm or partners (especially after the introduction of self assessment) may become insolvent when the liability is crystallised.

A firm is unable to adopt a cash basis of accounting until it has completed three years of trading. Thereafter, with the permission of their Inspector of Taxes, a switch can be made from a true earnings basis to a conventional basis. Upon such a transition there is a danger that some profits will be assessed twice. This happens because profits will have been recognised on the earnings basis but some of these profits will only be received as cash after this time and hence will lead to double assessment on the change to the conventional basis. This tax disadvantage has to be weighed against the benefit of the tax deferral advantage that is created by operating on a cash basis.

A new firm with relatively low profits may only suffer relatively few double assessments on a change of accounting basis especially as, in the early days, the only fee earners are likely to be the partners (see below), and this may be totally inconsequential as a firm grows when put against the benefits to cash flow of deferring tax liabilities until later dates by adopting a cash basis of accounting.

Firms that adopt an earnings basis and therefore account for work in progress have agreed a wide range of methods for calculating a work in progress value with the Inland Revenue. Work in progress should be valued at the lower of cost and net realisable value and unless time is being written off, this means work in progress should normally be valued at cost.

Time spent by fee earners on an unbilled file should be valued using charge-out rates that are being used at the time minus any profit element that is included within these charge-out rates. It is important to note that the Inland Revenue has accepted that partners have zero cost in that there is no expense to be charged against fee income for their time. Partner time can therefore legitimately be discounted in determining the work in progress figure at the year end and hence in determining taxable profits. Such a method of valuation does in effect understate the value of the work in progress and partners must therefore be happy with this method of valuation before it is adopted. Reducing the work in progress valuation in this way will defer tax liabilities and defer profits and hence reduce pressure on partner drawings until such time as the profit is realised as cash. Obviously, a full earnings basis (to include partners' time) could be adopted if the partnership agrees.

Borrowing

The borrowings that are necessary to provide partnership capital may be personal borrowings, borrowings of the partnership or a combination of both. Provided that the borrowings are for the business (wholly and exclusively) then the interest on both types of loan will be tax deductible. For personal loans, tax relief is available if claimed through the individual partner's tax return. Partnership borrowings, which tend to be for the provision of working capital, are claimed through the accounts and partnership return. There is also a difference between the two types of borrowings when one considers the effect on pension provision. Borrowings in the partnership result in interest charges paid by the partnership and give rise to a reduction in net relevant earnings which are used to calculate the amount of pension contributions that partners can make in each year. However, for personal loans taken out to finance partnership capital, the interest on these loans is tax deductible, but does not affect net relevant earnings and hence such loans mean that partners may be able to contribute larger amounts in a tax efficient manner into pension schemes.

It might therefore appear sensible to arrange for all borrowings to be undertaken by partners individually but in practice this may not be possible and certainly will not be possible on the most commercially beneficial terms. For example, 30 partners borrowing £100,000 each are unlikely to obtain as good a rate of interest as the partnership as a whole borrowing the money on behalf of all of the partners. This saving in terms of interest paid may well be worth more to the individual partners concerned than the additional pension contributions that can be made within each year.

It is important when preparing accounts for a solicitors' firm to ensure that a distinction is kept between the partners' capital and current accounts. A partner's capital account represents the liability of the partnership to repay an individual partner the capital that has been contributed to the firm while the balance on a current account shows any undistributed profits at any point in time. Current accounts can become overdrawn when drawings exceed profits earned. It is important to keep capital accounts and current accounts separate so that if at any stage a current account becomes temporarily overdrawn this cannot be deemed by the Revenue to be a repayment of capital. If such an event could be deemed a repayment of capital then tax relief on any borrowings associated with the provision of this capital would be restricted.

Consider a situation for a partner who has contributed £50,000 of capital and in their first year as a partner has earned £60,000 but had drawings of £65,000. If capital accounts and current accounts are kept separately then, at the end of the year, the partner would have a balance on a capital account of £50,000 and an overdrawn current account of £5,000. If, however, there had been no distinction between capital and current accounts then at the end of year one the total capital accounts could show a balance of £45,000 and hence a repayment of some of the original £50,000 of capital introduced. The ability for tax relief to be claimed on the £50,000 of borrowings would be lost.

It is important that partners always try to ensure that tax relief is obtained on borrowings equal to the amount of capital that has been contributed into the partnership. Consider the situation where a new partner borrows £50,000 personally and contributes this capital into the partnership for a qualifying purpose. In the first year, any interest paid on the £50,000 of capital will be tax deductible and effectively reduce taxable profits. In the second year the firm disposes of part of the business and in addition to trading profits, makes a capital profit per partner of £25,000. The firm might take such an opportunity to retain this £25,000 as additional capital to finance expansion of the firm rather than to distribute this profit out by way of drawings. As a result of these steps the partner now has just £50,000 borrowings but £75,000 worth of capital within the partnership. Assuming that the partner also has other private loans which are not tax deductible, for example a large mortgage on a main residence, it would make sense to refinance and transfer some of the borrowings out of the main residence and into the partnership. To achieve this goal the partnership could pay £50,000 out to pay off the partner's personal borrowings and a further £25,000 to extinguish part of the mortgage on the main residence. On the same day, the bank could provide £75,000 of capital to the partnership as partnership capital, in effect transferring borrowings on the main residence to partnership borrowings. Following these transactions the partner will now be able to deduct the interest paid on all £75,000 of partnership capital from taxable profit. It has to be pointed out that there are two major areas of concern here.

(a)   Self assessment transitional rules — the anti-avoidance rules for the 1996/97 year indicate that if partnership borrowings are replaced by private drawings during the transitional period and this is not being done for bona fide commercial reasons, the advantage gained will be eliminated.

(b)   Tax anti-avoidance legislation (Income and Corporation Taxes Act 1988, s. 787) which indicates that where a loan is taken out to obtain a tax advantage, this advantage can be eliminated! Generally this provision is not applied to refinancing partnerships.

Deciding on the right year end for tax purposes — self assessment

This chapter is not meant to be a technical treatise on taxation. However, a book written in 1996 cannot pass without mention of the new self assessment rules and their effect on solicitors' accounts and partnerships.

The first point to note is that as the mechanism for raising assessments to collect tax from the partnership disappears so joint liability for partners' tax disappears! Another basic point to note is that from 1997/98 onwards for all existing partnerships (from 6 April 1994 for new partnerships), including those with partnership changes where no continuation elections have been submitted, so long as there is at least one individual partner remaining in the partnership before and after a change (i.e., including from sole practitioner to partnership or from partnership to sole practitioner) the partnership will be required to submit a return and will be treated as a continuing entity. Each partner will, however, be taxed effectively as a sole practitioner within the confines of the partnership accounts. Accordingly there will be no need for the partnership agreement to contain any provisions regarding continuation elections as no such elections will be needed. This concept of each partner being taxed as a sole practitioner within the confines of the partnership means that each partner will be taxed on the opening and closing rules applied to the profits and profit sharing ratio shown in the partnership accounts for the appropriate periods of membership, not fiscal years of membership. It is also necessary to consider how the partnership changes from old prior year basis to the new current year basis. Figure 26 shows a numerical example of the transitional year but then, more importantly, the situation on the admission and retirement of partners illustrating this new concept.

Figure 26   XYZ

X and Y have been in partnership for many years. They make their accounts up to 30 June. X is reaching retirement age. Y cannot run the practice himself and wants an orderly transfer of goodwill and so, on 1 July 2001, Z joins the partnership and on 30 April 2003 X retires. Profits are shared equally. For the early years the figures are:

Year	Profits Assessment	Year of Profits	Assessable
		£	£
30 June 1994	20,000	1995/96	20,000
20 June 1995	(25,000)	1996/97	25,000
30 June 1996	(25,000)	(transitional year)	
30 June 1997	30,000	1997/98	30,000

The transitional year will be taxed on the profit sharing ratio of the fiscal year and the tax will be collected mainly via a composite partnership assessment. Credit for these interim payments is then given to individual partners for their sweep up payments on 31 January 1998 when the 1996/97 tax return is submitted.

The transitional overlap relief is given for the period 1 July 1996 to 5 April 1997, i.e., $9/12 \times £30,000 = £22,500$ or £11,250 each.

On 1 July 2001 Z joins the partnership and on 30 April 2003 X retires. For the later years, the figures are:

		£
30 June 2001	profits	40,000
30 June 2002	profits	60,000
30 June 2003	profits	90,000

Which will be assessed as follows:

	X	Y	Z
2001/2	£20,000	£20,000	£45,000 x 1/3
			£15,000 (note 1)
2002/3	£20,000	£20,000	£20,000
2003/4	£13,750	£32,500 (note 2)	£32,500

Note 1:   X and Y are taxed on their 50% profit share of 30 June 2001 whereas Z is taxed in 2001/02 on the profits arising in the period 1 July 2001 to 5 April 2002. The profits are $3/4 \times £60,000$.

These 9 months' worth of profits are taxed again in the following year's assessment and so give the overlap period to carry forward to his cessation or an earlier extended period of account.

Note 2:   X is taxed on the period 1 July 2002 to 30 April 2003, i.e., 10/12 of his share of £90,000 less transitional relief of £11,250.

It should be remembered that from 1996/97 onwards partnership returns will be issued for completion. All the normal penalties for late submission of returns etc. are geared up by the number of partners. Assume therefore the partnership return issued to X, Y and Z for 2002/3 is submitted on 7 February 2004 (a week late!) there will be an automatic penalty of £400!

Another important difference is that it would not be possible for partners to claim personal expenses or capital allowances on their own tax returns. For 1996/97 onwards unless such personal expenses are included upon the partnership return no relief can be obtained for them. Partnership profits can subsequently be allocated to ensure the partners receive credit for their underlying expenses but for this to happen the partners must be aware of their reporting duties. It is suggested therefore that as partnership deeds are amended to remove provisions concerning continuation elections, clauses are inserted to ensure that partners know that unless their personal expenses are reported to the partnership secretary within certain time limits they will not be included upon the partnership return and therefore they would not be able to obtain relief.

Where the partnership receives other income such as rent from surplus office accommodation or client account interest then the taxation treatment can be complex. Where the rent is received from surplus office accommodation it is important to establish with the inspector that this is merely temporary, in which case the Revenue generally accept that the income is not schedule A income but can be taxed within the schedule D Case II computations and no further adjustments are required. With client accounts, where the partnership retains beneficial ownership of the interest then generally, as long as the partners receive benefit in the same proportions that they receive their schedule D Case II profits then client account interest, whilst a separate taxable source of income, is dealt with not on a fiscal year basis but in an identical fashion to the professional profits making life a lot simpler. The same will apply to any schedule A income where this is received in the same profit sharing ratio as the professional partnership. Unfortunately with solicitors, this is seldom the case and to the extent that the capital sharing ratio on a particular property differs from the profit sharing ratio for the professional partnership, a different 'partnership' exists for each such property which must send in partnership returns on a fiscal year basis.

On submission of the partnership return and satisfaction of the normal audit requirements, the partnership's taxation duties are at an end. Each partner will be provided as part of the partnership return with a statement of his or her assessable profits for each particular year. It will therefore be up to the partner to ensure that this information is included on their own self assessment return. It is also up to the partner to make the appropriate payments on account on 31 January in the tax year and 31 July following the tax year (based on the liability of the previous year) and then the final sweep up of payment on 31 January following the end of the tax year when the appropriate self assessment return is submitted. As indicated above, joint liability for taxation disappears but partners will have a continuing interest in ensuring that their colleagues keep up to date for, if an entry on a self assessment return has a knock on effect on the partnership leading to increased taxation being paid by the partnership as a whole, the appropriate surcharges and penalties are levied on each partner within that partnership.

Historically, under the prior year basis of assessment, most firms chose 30 April year ends as this resulted in the maximum deferral of tax liabilities. Under the prior year basis of assessment the profits assessed in a particular tax year were the profits earned in the accounting period ending in the previous fiscal year. For example, for a firm with an April year end the profits assessed for tax in the year ending on 5 April 1994 would be profits earned in the accounting period ending in 30 April 1992, these being the profits of the accounts ending in the tax year ending 5 April 1993.

With the basis of assessment moving to a current year basis of assessment, profits in a particular tax year are assessed by reference to the profits of the accounting period ending in the current tax year. A 30 April year end therefore still results in the greatest deferral, although this deferral is reduced from the deferral that was present under the prior year basis of assessment due to the way interim payments on account are required.

Under the current year basis of assessment, some profits will be taxed twice in the early years or on a change of accounting date and these double taxed profits are eventually relieved through what is called overlap relief (see Figure 27). Generally overlap relief will only be used on the cessation of a partnership or on the retirement of a particular partner. All partners who obtain overlap relief (either when the partnership changed from the previous year basis to the current year basis through the 1996/97 transitional year or on commencement (if appropriate)) will find that over the years this overlap relief becomes very small compared with the future levels of profit, given that there is likey to be some inflation, increasing profits within the firm and that individual partners will be expecting to be promoted to higher shares of profits in the future. Also, the rules on cessation can lead to more than 12 months' profit being assessed in the year of retirement (e.g., retirement on 31 March 1999 where accounts are drawn up to 30 April means that the 1998/99 assessment is based on all the profits accruing from 1 May 1997 to 31 March 1999, a total of 23 months (before overlap relief!)). This is often called the 'bunching' effect.

Given the above state of affairs there is a danger that the final tax liability payable by partners may not be fully appreciated by the partners until they actually retire. Firms should therefore consider making provision for the extra final tax liabilities during the working life of partners so that there is no final shock on retirement. The worst scenario that can be envisaged is one where a partner retires thinking he or she has sufficient funds for retirement, only to find that on receiving the final tax liability he or she either has to use the pension commutation or has to return to work for a further period! Provision for this extra tax liability can be charged to a partner's current account in each year to result in additional partners' capital in the balance sheet and is therefore doubly attractive. If partners' profit shares are not increased, or indeed if profits do not increase, then it will not be necessary to make this additional provision, nor will it be necessary if the date of retirement is chosen with care and an accounts year end late in the tax year is adopted. However, if an early year end is preferred to obtain the maximum tax deferral an example of the way reserves could be built up is shown in Figure 27.

Many firms have decided with the advent of the current year basis of assessment to switch the year end to 31 March. While this means that there is now the lowest possible deferral of tax liabilities the tax picture is kept much simpler in that tax affairs are always up to date with the profits earned to 31 March being assessed in the same year to 5 April.

Figure 27   Partner's tax reserve

It is assumed that in the accounts to 30 April 1995, a partner's profit is £100,000. This is likely to increase at 5% per annum until they retire on 30 April 2005 (as required to do under the partnership agreement). If the partnership is worried about the bunching effect on retirement, a change of accounting date to 31 March could be the solution, in which case this is probably best done during the transitional period, say to 31 March 1997 from 30 April 1996. The profits will be in each of the alternatives therefore:

Year ended:	£		£
30 April 1995	100,000		
30 April 1996	105,000		
30 April 1997	110,250	1 May 1996 — 31 Mar 1997	101,063
30 April 1998	115,762	31 Mar 1998	115,302
30 April 1999	121,551	31 Mar 1999	121,069
30 April 2000	127,628	31 Mar 2000	127,125
30 April 2001	134,009	31 Mar 2001	133,477
30 April 2002	140,710	31 Mar 2002	140,151
30 April 2003	147,745	31 Mar 2003	147,158
30 April 2004	155,133	31 Mar 2004	154,518
30 April 2005	162,889	31 Mar 2005	162,243
		1 April — 30 April 2005	14,253

This would be taxed over the appropriate years as follows:

Year of Assessment		30 April year end £	31 March year end £
1996/97	Note 1	102,500	105,121
1997/98	Note 2	110,250	115,302
1998/99		115,762	121,069
1999/00		121,551	127,125
2000/01		127,628	133,477
2001/02		134,009	140,151
2002/03		140,710	147,158
2003/04		147,745	154,518
2004/05		155,133	162,243
2005/06	Note 3	61,826	14,253
		£1,217,114	£1,220,417

Note 1:   Transitional year (£100,000 + £105,000) × 12/24 = £102,500

(£100,000 + £105,000 + £101,603) × 12/35 = £105,121

Note 2:   Overlap relief for 30 April year end

£110,250 × 11/12 = £101,063

Note 3:   Cessation profits for 30 April year end

£162,889 − overlap relief of £101,063 = £61,826

From the above details there are three items of interest:

(a)   The 31 March year end accelerates the time at which tax becomes due on about £6,000 of profits on average.

(b)   The 31 March year end produces a slightly higher tax charge overall.

(c)   The final year's liability will be about 4 times larger for the 30 April year end due to the erosion over time of the overlap relief.

However, this could easily be provided for on an ongoing basis. Many formulae could be used but a suggestion is:

(Partner's profit share × overlap period) − overlap relief

This would give the necessary reserve at any one moment in time but could be accumulated each year. This is demonstrated below:

Year end		Deferred profits	Required reserve at marginal rate of tax (say 40%)	Transfer to reserve
		£	£	£
30 April 1997	Note 1	NIL	NIL	NIL
30 April 1998	Note 2	5,052	2,000	2,000
30 April 1999	Note 3	10,359	4,100	2,100
30 April 2000		15,929	6,300	2,200
30 April 2001		21,779	8,700	2,400
30 April 2002		27,921	11,100	2,400
30 April 2003		34,370	13,700	2,600
30 April 2004		41,142	16,400	2,700
30 April 2005		48,252	19,300	2,900
				£19,300

Note 1: No transfer required as overlap.
Note 2: (£115,762 × 11/12) − £101,063 = £5,052
Note 3: (£121,551 × 11/12) − £101,063 = £10,359

So when the partner retires on 30 April 2005 and is faced with a tax liability of about £25,000, there is a reserve of £19,300 to help settle it, compared with the 31 March alternative of £5,700 and no reserves, i.e., he or she has adequately reserved this exceptional liability.

Service companies

An increasing but still fairly small number of firms are establishing service companies which are owned by the partnership. While there may be some additional costs incurred in operating a separate company, partnerships do not normally need to be very large before the other benefits outlined in this section outweigh any incremental costs which are incurred.

A service company will pay tax on any profits earned at corporation tax rates of tax as opposed to the profits of the partnership which will suffer income tax at income tax rates. Corporation tax rates are generally lower than income tax rates, for example in the year to 5 April 1997 the full rate of corporation tax was 33%, the small companies rate of corporation tax was 24% on profits up to £300,000 while income tax was payable at 40% for partners earning taxable profits in excess of £24,300. Where a firm is looking to accumulate capital, for whatever purpose, it is therefore more tax efficient to do so in a company than in a partnership. For example, if a firm wishes to acquire a new computer system or is to establish a new business then it will be more tax efficient to accumulate the capital within a company than within the partnership.

Two other advantages accrue from the use of service companies. These are as follows:

(a)   Where disallowables are incurred such as entertaining or depreciation (i.e., holding many of the partnership fixed assets in the company), it is sensible for these to be incurred by the service company and then to be recharged as part of the total undivided management charge to the partnership. Here the disallowance is likely to be at the marginal rate of tax of the company — probably 24% compared with the partners' marginal rate of tax at 40%.

(b)   Where expensive cars are purchased by the partners which have substantial business usage, consideration should be given to the service company purchasing the car and then transferring it to the partnership after about 1 year. As the transactions are between connected parties, an election could be made for the asset to be transferred at tax written down value but it is suspected that for the average type of car balancing allowances will arise which can lead to a substantial acceleration of allowances as the attached example shows.

Figure 28 Car

A car worth £25,000 is purchased for a partner by a service company on 1 July 1996 with a year end of 31 May 1997. This is transferred on 30 April 1997 to the partnership (where the year end is 30 April):

Capital allowance treatment:

in company to 31 May 1997	Expensive car £
Addition	25,000
Less disposal proceeds (Market Value)	19,000
Balancing allowance	£6,000

In partnership for 1997/98

	Expensive car £	Private use 40% £	Allowances £
Addition at Market Value	19,000		
Written down allowance @ 25% (but restricted)	3,000	1,200	1,800
Written down value carried forward	16,000		

Had the car been purchased directly by the partnership then the total allowance available to the partnership for the same period would have been £1,800 (as compared with £7,800 as above!).

Obviously the P11D implications must not be forgotten but a one off tax advantage should be available. A P11D is the end of year return submitted by the employer to the Inland Revenue, which details reimbursed expenses and benefits in kind of higher paid employees.

These service companies can also be used as a way of distributing income to the spouses of partners and as a consequence, often paying lower rates of tax. In a successful firm, a large proportion of the profits earned will be taxable at

119

40%. If a proportion of the profits are earned within a company and this company is owned by the partners then the dividend income distributed will also be taxed at 40%. It is possible, however, to transfer some of the ownership of the company to spouses, perhaps through the use of preference shares. Provided that the spouses do not already have significant personal income, the dividend income earned by the spouses will only be assessed at the basic or lower rate of income tax. Care should be taken on the creation of the second class of shares so that the Revenue are not tempted to try to invoke the settlement rules. This could lead to the Revenue arguing that the creation and subsequent lift (transfer of shares) to the non-working spouse constituted the creation of a settlement which would lead to the dividends being taxed back on the settler or donor. Despite this threat, the scheme may be used so long as commerciality prevails (i.e., odd share rights such as variable dividends or voting rights should be avoided).

A service company can also be used in connection with a Funded Unapproved Retirement Benefits Scheme (FURBS) (see below).

Even with the availability of a more flexible pension policy (see below) partners may consider that they have made inadequate provision for their retirement. To the extent that profit is retained within a service company then it could be considered that a salary could be paid to directors (partners) for services provided, in which case a small self administered pension scheme (SSAS) could be established. However, in view of the fact that a partner tends to work full time for the partnership (as required by the partnership agreement), this makes it difficult for the company to pay a sufficient salary to the partner which would allow reasonable pension contributions to the SSAS.

There has been correspondence between the Pension Schemes Office (PSO) and the various professional bodies indicating that the salaries that they would accept to qualify for pension payments into such a scheme would be modest (£500 in 1978!). If it is decided that a SSAS would not be convenient, the interim measure of an executive pension plan (EPP) should be considered. Should incorporation of professional partnerships arise prior to the retirement of the partners, it would be possible for an EPP to be evolved into a SSAS once the partners became full time directors upon incorporation. Maximum flexibility would thus have been achieved.

The amounts involved with either EPPs or SSAS currently are small and it is not clear when incorporation may or may not arise. Should it be desired that larger amounts be placed within a company pension scheme then the FURB route must be adopted. FURBS arose subsequent to the introduction of capping on traditional pension policies. Where a partner is either over funded on his pension provision or is capped to the amount they can put in, consideration should be given to a FURB. Here the contributions can be made effectively without limit (from a pension premium point of view) although deductibility for Schedule D Case 1 purposes should always be considered. As the payments are into an unapproved retirement benefit scheme the funds are not tied up long term and can be loaned back to the company in the interim. Unfortunately, as the schemes are unapproved, the premiums will be a P11D benefit for the director/partner and the fund will not accrue tax free. However, the fund will be taxed at slightly preferential rates (34%) compared with the partners' marginal rate of tax (40%) and a lump sum, which is tax free, can be extracted on retirement. Also, as a P11D benefit, there are no National Insurance contributions to worry about, which makes it a very tax efficient form of cash extraction. The final advantage of a FURB in this brief description is that the retirement date is not defined and this leads to increased flexibility.

Financial services

It should not be forgotten that a service company could also be used to earn income through financial services advice. Historically it was not possible for firms to keep any commissions that were earned through financial services business unless clients gave their express permission for firms to keep such commissions. The rules have now changed and provided profits are earned through a separate company or joint venture which does not bear the name of the partnership, then it is possible for that company to retain the commissions earned. The profits earned from such activities once earned in the service company can then benefit from some of the savings outlined above.

Profit related pay

Profit related pay schemes were established as a government device for increasing the generation of wealth by encouraging entities to share any additional profits earned with the staff who helped in the creation of those profits. The schemes allow employees to earn some or all of these profit contributions as tax free income (the lesser of £4,000 or 20% of pay) with the balance (if any) being chargeable. The requirement was that to qualify as tax free PRP, it was necessary for some or all of that pay to be linked to the profits of the business.

Profit related pay schemes could be established within a partnership but under the PRP rules, all schemes must have their accounts audited. Audits would not normally be performed on the results for a partnership so this could give rise to problems with secrecy and more worryingly on SSAP 9 valuations of work in progress! The normal route in professional firms is to operate the profit related pay scheme through a separate company which could be the service company outlined in the above sections. Staff are employed by a separate service company and their services are sold back to the partnership on the basis of an agreed formula which is acceptable to the Inland Revenue. Generally this route will not be acceptable for smaller partnerships (less than 10 partners). The formula for the service charge cannot be a straight cost plus margin but must have an element of dependence upon the results (say the turnover) of the partnership. Some of the profits earned by this service company are then distributed to staff in addition to the basic salaries through a PRP scheme. It is usually possible to structure these schemes in such a way that staff will receive a bonus (which will be tax free) in addition to their basic salary which would continue unless the firm itself were to get into severe financial difficulty verging on bankruptcy. The anti-avoidance rules stopping salary sacrifices would not normally apply in these circumstances but cannot be ignored. The employment law issues must also not be ignored.

Given that profit relies on generating any marginal income that can be earned and controlling marginal costs as effectively as possible, the establishment of a profit related pay scheme that involves all staff is likely to have a positive effect over the medium to long term. In a solicitors' firm, great care must be taken to consider the 'permitted' adjustment to the profits for PRP purposes to increase the linkage between people's actions and profitability. The government have announced in the November 1996 Budget that PRP schemes are to be completely phased out by 1999/2000.

The service charge

Care should be taken in establishing the quantum of the service charge. It is vital from a direct taxation point of view that the amount remains consistently calculated between years. The quantum should also be commercially justifiable. Where the staff are transferred from partnership to service company then the cost plus method element referred to above should not be excessive. There is sufficient case law in the Revenue's favour to indicate that a profit loading in the region of 5 to 10% would probably be acceptable in most circumstances. The greater the commercial risk undertaken by the service company the higher the profit loading that the Revenue will accept. It makes sense therefore also to include other services which may be charged for, such as debt factoring and the provision of fixed assets to give the company a real commercial substance, as well as maybe routing the provision of financial services through the company although consideration should be given to putting the financial services business through a separate company for regulatory reasons. Consideration should also be given to the fact that the service company is a close company and so great care should be taken on any intercompany/partnership charges that such debts are settled on a commercial basis (in any case within the normal 6 month rule) or there may be a s. 419, Income and Corporation Taxes Act 1988 problem (notional ACT on the non-commercial loans).

Consideration should also be given to the VAT treatment of the service charge. The provision of management services to the group is chargeable at the standard rate. However, a planning point does arise in that the service company should not have its year end coterminus with the partnership so that its VAT quarters would not be likely to coincide with those of the partnership. A timing advantage can therefore be extracted on the management fee by timing the raising of the appropriate invoices just after the VAT quarter of the service company but just prior to the VAT quarter of the partnership. To the extent that the business relates to financial services it may well be exempt. Care must be taken therefore to watch partial exemption rules.

Retirement planning in solicitors' partnerships

The normal rule is that the payments into approved pension contracts, whether they be personal pension plans or retirement annuity contracts, will be tax deductible at the highest marginal rate of personal taxation. There are limits to the amount which can be contributed in any year, these limits being determined by the amount of net relevant earnings ('NRE') and a percentage of these earnings which increases with age. The system therefore encourages pension provision throughout the working life but provides tax breaks which increase as a person approaches retirement. The earlier that contributions are made into these pension schemes the better, since this allows for a longer period of growth within the scheme before pensions are drawn and hence means that the cost of providing a certain pension is cheaper than if contributions are deferred until a later date. One reason for this is that approved pension schemes operate entirely free of tax with no tax being paid on income or gains of the pension scheme.

On retirement the income which is drawn from a pension scheme will be taxable at the marginal rate of tax although a tax free lump sum may be taken at the time of drawing a pension.

Pension payments are fully tax deductible and pension funds grow in a tax free environment so pension planning must always be near the top of the list of tax planning ideas for solicitors. Recent changes to pension legislation have meant that pensions can now be drawn as early as the age of 50 and hence pension planning is not necessarily such a long term investment.

Pension planning can also be used as a way of providing capital for a partnership more tax efficiently than is often the case. Consider initially the situation where a partner borrows £50,000 personally which is then contributed to the partnership as partnership borrowings. Under these circumstances the partner is able to claim tax relief for the interest payable on the £50,000 loan each year but there is no tax relief for the contribution to the partnership itself. However, arrangements could be established for a partner to borrow £50,000 and to pay this sum into a personal pension scheme. The payment of £50,000 into a personal pension scheme could be fully deductible at the highest marginal rate of income tax of 40% for the entire contribution making the net cost just £30,000. The pension scheme could then loan an element of the £50,000 back to the partnership. While the partner would now not get tax relief from the original borrowings, the partnership would get tax relief on any interest paid on the loan from the pension fund (which would not be taxable in the fund). In this method capital is provided to the partnership and full tax relief is given on the contribution of that capital.

Alternative methods based on a similar method can be negotiated with pension companies. It may be decided that partners will put some or all of their pension contributions into one particular pension scheme as agreed between the partners, and that this pension scheme will invest the funds within cash deposits. Tax relief therefore is obtained upon contributions under the normal Retirement Annuity Premiums (RAP) Personal Pension rules. However, as the funds are in the form of cash deposits it will be possible (subject to negotiation between the life office and a clearing bank) to use these deposits to enable the partnership to have loan facilities equal to the cash deposits (effectively through a back-to-back arrangement). Therefore as the funds within the scheme increase, so the facility for working capital increases within the partnership, effectively providing the partnership with an additional source of working capital.

Partners will not always wish to tie up funds in pension funds for such long periods either for personal reasons or because it is appreciated that the partnership may need to obtain more cash in the short term and therefore other financial planning products may be more appropriate. While other products may receive some tax benefits in terms of suffering little or no tax on income and gains there is no other type of investment that gives such good tax relief on the original investment.

Identification of non-professional or trading income

'Trading' profits of a firm give rise to profits that are used for net relevant earnings calculations and it is the net relevant earnings of a particular partner that are the basis for the amount of pension contributions that could be made within a particular year. It is therefore important to ensure that net relevant earnings are as high as possible, although once the net relevant earnings cap has been reached this becomes less significant. Non-trading income does not constitute net relevant earnings and it will be useful for firms to try to 'convert' any such non-trading income into trading income. For example, the interest earned on client account balances would be investment income but could be converted into practice income if a set-off is arranged with a bank by which no interest is earned on non-designated client account balances but reduced overdraft interest is paid on practice account balances. Great care must be adopted so that the bank understands exactly what is proposed. Many so called 'offsets' have been agreed with the bank but when the bank statements have been scrutinised there is the bank interest received shown on the statement and then a contra entry against the loan account! Undertaken successfully, this will not only have the effect of increasing net relevant earnings but will also increase profits generally, because the marginal cost of borrowing is normally higher than the rate of interest earned on deposits.

When office space is rented out, the income generated should be treated as surplus accommodation and negotiations with the Revenue completed so that the income is taxed under schedule DII rather than schedule A (see section on self assessment).

Capital gains tax and retirement relief

The caveat given that this chapter is not a detailed tax manual is especially the case for this section! The basic capital gains tax legislation was not designed to cope with partnerships. What little legislation there is has been tacked on to provide a basic charging mechanism. Further, there is little case law on which reliance can be placed to expand and enhance this area. Therefore it is necessary to look at Revenue practice. A number of very comprehensive statements of practice have been published over the years dealing with partnership taxation and these should always be considered when reviewing a solicitors practice.

Generally transactions between partners will give rise to capital gains tax consequences. Despite the fact that usually partners are connected with each other for tax purposes, these connected party rules are ignored unless there is a more immediate relationship (such as family) for transactions between partners. Thus, for the purposes of computing capital gains, the consideration given at the time of the partnership change or on a change in capital sharing ratio is:

(a) if the partners make a bargain — whatever the consideration that bargain provides;

(b) if the partners make no particular bargain — whatever value is attributed to the asset in the balance sheet at the time of the change (including revaluations!);

(c) if there is no value placed on the item on the balance sheet and there is no bargain then nil consideration is attributed to the transaction.

The interaction between the valuation placed on an asset on the balance sheet and events that lead to capital gains tax consequences outlined in (b) above, gives rise to the complexity of capital taxes in partnership. Generally large professional partnerships have decided to abolish goodwill payments because new partners cannot afford to purchase goodwill. If that is the case then where a partner has paid for goodwill which is subsequently abolished, a negligible value claim could be submitted to crystallise the capital loss.

It is important to keep detailed records of the particular position of each partner in respect of each capital asset owned by the partnership, whether it be goodwill (if this is included upon the balance sheet) or any other capital assets such as offices, especially where they are revalued on retirements and admissions. Failure to do this can lead to substantial and unnecessary fees arising when a partner retires or joins, caused by having to prove that the consequent changes in profit sharing ratios applied to each asset (goodwill, property etc.) do not give rise to chargeable gains in excess of the annual exemptions.

With this in mind it is easy to see that in a professional partnership which recognises goodwill, substantial gains can arise on the retirement of a partner. As with income tax pension planning, this area of tax planning must not be ignored. It could easily be envisaged that in some solicitors practices, if goodwill were to be recognised at full market value, gains substantially in excess of the maximum levels of retirement relief could easily be in point. At that level, retirement relief is worth £250,000 in savings of tax (the first £250,000 being fully exempt plus 50% of the gains arising between £250,000 and £1,000,000). The relief is available from age 50 (55 to November 1995) or earlier on the grounds of ill health. Retirement relief is available to a partner on the following disposals:

(a)   the whole or part of a business;
(b)   the disposal of an asset which at the time the business ceased was used for the purposes of the business; or
(c)   an associated disposal (here the asset is owned by the individual partner and it is used for the partnership business and is disposed of within the appropriate time limits of the date of the retirement of that partner from the practice).

Therefore it is clear that mere disposals of assets do not qualify for retirement relief.

The following could give rise to problems (but the list is by no means exhaustive!).

(a)   The payment of rent for the occupation of the offices by a partnership to a partner who owns the offices (or a property owning partnership which could be a limited number of partners owning the practice property in different capital sharing ratios from the professional partners) which could also include the solicitors' practice paying the mortgage which is deemed rent — the payment of rent will lead to a restriction on the retirement relief available on gains arising on those particular premises.

(b)   The retention by partners of their share of particular properties after retiring from the solicitors' practice — if the remaining partners are unable to buy the partner out of his or her share of the property on retirement, he or she must be warned that retirement relief would not be available to cover any gains arising after retirement from the partnership. It would be better to crystallise the sale and take a charge over the property.

(c)   Capital accounts held within the partnership after retirement — as with property these will cease to be counted as business assets where it is clear that under the partnership deed the money has to be kept in there effectively as an investment for a number of years.

(d)   Partial retirements — although the legislation can cope with partial retirements, great care should be taken. As stated above, retirement relief is available on the disposal of all or part of a business. In theory therefore it would be possible for a partner to dispose of a substantial proportion of his or her goodwill in one year, claim retirement relief on that and then retire fully a couple of years later. However, due to the particular case law, it is unlikely that, in those circumstances, the 'interference test' would have been satisfied (i.e., did the disposal of goodwill so interfere with the business being undertaken that it afterwards became a different business?) so then retirement relief would not be available. If, however, the disposal in point was an entire office as a self contained unit but the retention of another, then relief may be available. Likewise, the disposal of, say, the conveyancing section of the practice but the continuation of the trust and probate section, could give rise to retirement relief on the gain arising on the conveyancing side.

(e) Where the shares are held by the partners in service companies, financial services companies etc., it is unlikely that retirement relief would be available on any gains arising on the disposal of those shares. The key criteria for the availability for retirement relief on the disposal of shares are that:

(i)   the requisite number of shares are held (5%); and
(ii)   the shareholder is a full time working director or employee.

The Revenue have long held the view that a partner in a professional firm cannot be a partner and full time working director at the same time. This has recently been endorsed by the Special Commissioners on the sale by a chartered accountant of his shares in the firm's service company. There, retirement relief was denied to the retiring partner.

Inheritance tax and business property relief

On the death of a partner, their partnership and associated assets will need to be valued and included within their estate at death. As with capital gains tax, what the partnership deed states as to the valuation of assets, especially goodwill, will be important.

Business property relief should, however, be available on such assets at the full 100% rate unless the asset is owned personally by the partner and used by the partnership, in which case the rate will be 50%. However the normal caveats apply:

(a) As with retirement relief, on retirement capital accounts and property will eventually become investment assets and therefore be exposed to inheritance tax.

(b) Binding contracts for sale within the partnership agreement could lead to the denial of business property relief. Many partnership deeds contain clauses that require the executors to sell and the surviving partners to buy the deceased partner's share at valuation or in accordance with a formula. This according to the Inland Revenue gives rise to a binding contract for sale and therefore bars the estate from business property relief. Cross options avoid this problem so long as the option periods are not coterminus.

(c)   Partnership insurance — many partnerships pay for insurance to protect either the partnership or the parties' estate in the event of their death. The treatment of the premiums and subsequent reliefs is complex. However, so long as the policy is written in trust when it is to protect the estate of deceased, the receipts should not fall into the estate for IHT purposes.

Index

Advertising   103
Annual budget   27–8
  overheads   33
Annual financial cycle   25
Appraisals   83–4
Assistant solicitors
  allocation of time, annual   45–6
  chargeable hours   42–3, 44
  charge-out rates   47, 49
  motivation   77
  numbers   40

Bad debts   12
Balance sheets, projected   34
Billing, increasing speed of issue   57
Body language   99, 104–5
Borrowings
  reasons for   56
  tax planning   108–10
Brochures   102–3
Budgets
  annual   27–8, 33
  annual financial cycle   25
  cash flow forecast   34
  delegation giving clear budgets   81
  fee income budget   28–30
  individual tailored budgets   25–6
  individual targets   25
  management information   26
  master budgets   20–7
  overheads budget   32–4
  professional staff costs budget   30–2

Budgets — *continued*
  projected balance sheet from   34
  responsibility for achieving   25
  training   24, 97–8
  *see also each type of budget as main
    heading*
Business plans   16–34
  budgets *see* Budgets
  insolvency, reasons for *see* Insolvency
Business property relief   128–9

Capital
  investment appraisal   62–4
  return on   62
  working *see* Working capital control
Capital accounts   127
Capital gains tax   125–8
Cars   118, 119
Cash collection, speeding up   57
Cash flow
  discounted   63–4
  forecast   34
Chargeable hours   37, 39
  assistant solicitors   42–3, 44
  industrial average   42–6
  legal executives   43
  paralegals   43
  partners   42
  trainee solicitors   43
Charge-out rates   37, 39
  fee income budget preparation   28
  industrial averages   47–50

Charge-out rates — *continued*
  recovery and 54
Client care 88–105
  changing procedures 96–7
  internal communications 93–5
  marketing strategy *see* Marketing
    strategy
  presentations *see* Presentations
  pricing *see* Pricing
  reality 88–93
  teamwork 93–4
  training *see* Marketing strategy
  see also Clients
Clients
  dissatisfied clients 89
  existing clients 89
  marketing to *see* Client care; Marketing
    strategy
  questionnaire 91, 92–3
  referrers 89–90, 104
  returners 89
  superpleasing 90
  troublemakers 89
Conferences 95
Confidentiality, management reporting
  65
Control
  poor, insolvency and 17
  working capital *see* Working capital
    control
Credit
  debtor days 59, 68, 70, 71
  see also Borrowings

Deadlines, delegation and 81
Debtor days 59, 68, 70, 71
Deferred revenue expenditure 14–15
Delays, between instruction and receipt of
  cash 57
Delegation 79–82
  abdication 80
  barriers to 80
  budgets 81
  clear instructions 80–1
  deadlines 81
  feedback 82
  motivation 82
  not letting go 80
  precise requirements 81

Depreciation 14
Discounted cashflow method, investment
  appraisal 63–4
Diversification, excessive 19–20

Earnings basis accounting 107–8
Executive pension plan 120
Expenditure
  deferred revenue 14–15
  optimum levels in overheads
    budget 33
  see also Overheads; Overheads budget

Fee income budget
  analysed between departments 28
  charge-out rates 28
  history and future performance 29
  optimistic and pessimistic 29–30
  other income 30
  responsibility allocation 30
  seasonal variations 29
Feedback
  appraisals 83–4
  delegation and 82
  marketing campaign 94–5
Financial cycle 25
Financial services 121
Financial statements *see* Solicitor's
  accounts
Forecast
  cash flow 34
  see also Budgets
Funded Unapproved Retirement Benefits
  Scheme (FURBS) 120–1

Gearing 36–7, 39
  industrial averages 40–1
Goodwill 126, 127

Hierarchy of needs 77
Hours, chargeable *see* Chargeable
  hours
Hygiene factors 78

Income
  net relevant earnings 123, 125
  non-professional 125
  profit related pay 121–2
  trading 125

Inflation   31
  overheads   32
Information *see* Management reporting
Inheritance tax   128–9
Insolvency
  excessive diversification   19–20
  gross profit too low   17–18
  poor management control   17
  undercapitalisation   17
Insurance, death of partner   129
Investment appraisal   62–4
  discounted cashflow method   63–4
  partner agreement to investment   64
  payback method   63

Leadership   86–7
Legal executives   41
  chargeable hours   43
  charge-out rates   47, 49

Mailshots   102
Management control, poor, as insolvency
  cause   17
Management reporting   65–71
  actual information   66
  budget information   66
  confidentiality   65
  length   66, 67
  managing partners   65–6
  monthly information sheet   68
  personal performance   66
  preparation and use of information
    25, 26–7
  timeliness   66, 67
  training in use   66
Management skills
  business understanding   74–5
  commercial approach   74–5
  defined goals   74
  delegation   79–82
  feedback   82, 83–4
  leadership   86–7
  motivating   77–9
  organisation   75–6
  presentation skills   98–100
  significance   73
  supervision   82–3
  teamwork   84–6
  technical   76–7

Management skills — *continued*
  time management   75–6
Margin   38–9, 55
Marketing strategy   93
  advertising   103
  body language   104–5
  brochures   102–3
  feedback sheets   94–5
  industry specialisation   94
  internal communications   93–5
  mailshots   102
  presentation documents   103–4
  presentation skills   98–100
  pricing   100–1
  pricing *see* Pricing
  referrers   89–90, 104
  seminars   95
  service   94
  target area identification   96
  training
    budgets   97–8
    changing procedures   96–7
    culture   96
    presentation skills   98–100
    targets   97–8
Master budgets   20–7
  example   22–4
  interested parties   20–1, 25
  review meeting s   21
Motivational skills   77–9
  delegated work   82
  hierarchy of needs   77
  hygiene factors   78

Needs, hierarchy of   77
Net relevant earnings   123, 125
Non-professional income   125

Organisation skills   75–6
Overheads   10
Overheads budget
  general and sundry expenses   32
  greater analysis than annual budget
    33
  inflation   32
  last year   32
  longer term objectives   34
  optimum expenditure levels   33
  responsibility allocation   33–4

Paralegals 41
    chargeable hours 43
    charge-out rates 47, 49
Partial retirements 127-8
Partners
    allocation of time, annual 45
    chargeable hours 42
    charge-out rates 47, 49
    death insurance 129
    earnings as key to profitability 9-12
    investment agreement 64
    management skills *see* Management
        skills
    managing 65-6
    motivation 77, 79
    numbers 40
    taxation *see* Tax planning
Payback method, investment appraisal
    63
Pensions
    executive pension plan 120
    funded unapproved retirement benefits
        scheme (FURBS) 120-1
    net relevant earnings 123, 125
    retirement annuity premium personal
        pension rules 124
    self administered pension scheme
        120
    tax planning 108-9
Premises
    costs 10
    rent 127
Presentation documents 103-4
Presentation skills 98-100
    body language 99
    key skills 98-9
    needs of client 99
    rehearsal 98
Pricing
    free service 100-1
    pilot schemes 100-1
    undervalue 100
    value building 101
Prioritisation 76
Professional staff costs budget
    changes in staff structures 31
    costs in constituent parts 30-1
    inflation 31
    regional variations 31-2

Professional staff costs budget
    — *continued*
    responsibility allocation 31
Profit and loss account 6
    budgeted 34
    example 27
Profit related pay 121-2
Profitability
    bad debts 12
    client care and *see* Client care
    deferred revenue expenditure 14-15
    depreciation 14
    earnings of equity partners 9-12
    reasons 12-15
    rule of thumb 10
    survey of firms 11
    undercapitalisation 13
    work in progress 12-14

Recovery 37-8, 39
    charge-out rates and 54
    fixed fee situations 53
    industrial averages 50-5
    normal pattern 51
Referrers 89-90, 104
Retirement planning *see* Pensions
Retirement relief 126-7

Secretaries *see* Support staff
Self administered pension scheme 120
Seminars 95
Service companies 117-23
    advantages 118
    financial services 121
    profit related pay 121-2
    service charge 122-3
Skills, management *see* Management
    skills
Solicitors *see* Assistant solicitors;
    Partners; Trainee solicitors
Solicitors' accounts 3-8
    cash flow forecast 34
    expenditure 7-8
    profit and loss account 6, 27, 34
Staff structures 40
Supervision skills 82-3
Support staff 10
    appraisals 83-4
    motivation 79

Targets   97–8
  individual   25
Tax planning   106–29
  borrowing   108–10
  business property relief   128–9
  capital and current accounts   109
  capital gains tax   125–8
  cars   118, 119
  current year assessment   113–14
  financial services   121
  goodwill   126, 127
  inheritance tax   128–9
  non-professional income   125
  partial retirements   127–8
  partner's tax reserve   115
  partnership return   113
  pensions   108–9
    executive pension plan   120
    FURB   120–1
    net relevant earnings   123, 125
    planning   123–5
    retirement annuity premium personal
      pension rules   124
    self administered pension scheme
      120
  profit related pay   121–2
  rent payments   127
  retirement planning see pensions
  retirement relief   126–7
  self-assessment   110–17
  service companies   117–23
  spouses   119–20
  trading income   125
  work in progress valuation   107–8
  year end choice   113–17

Teamwork   84–6, 93–4
Technical skills   76–7
Time management   75–6
To Do List   75–6
Trading income   125
Trainee solicitors   41
  chargeable hours   43
  charge-out rates   47, 49
  motivation   77
Training   41
  budgets   24, 97–8
  changing procedures   96–7
  culture   96
  management information use   66
  management skills   73
  presentation skills   98–100
  seminars   95
  targets   97–8

Undercapitalisation   13
  insolvency cause   17

Work in progress
  accounting basis   107–8
  days   59, 61
  profitability and   12–14
  recovery   37–8
  tax planning   107–8
  valuation   12–13, 107–8
Working capital control   56–61
  dangerous times   59
  debtor days   59
  poor   58
  typical   58–9
  work in progress days   59, 61